Unlocking Your Career Potential

Jane Ballback
Jan Slater

KOGAN PAGE

First published in 1996 by Richard Chang Associates, Inc., USA.

This edition published in 1998 by Kogan Page

Kogan Page Limited
120 Pentonville Road
London N1 9JN

© 1996, Richard Chang Associates, Inc., Publications Division, 15265 Alton Parkway, Suite 300, Irvine, CA 92618, USA. (800) 756-8096 (714) 727-7477 Fax (714) 727-7007 www.richardchangassociates.com

British Library Cataloguing in Publication Data

A CIP record for this book is available from the British Library.

ISBN 0 7494 2665 9

Typeset in Great Britain by
Northern Phototypesetting Co Ltd, Bolton
Printed and bound in Great Britain by
Biddles Ltd, Guildford and King's Lynn

Acknowledgements

This book was fifteen years in the making. We kept waiting for the *right* time to begin the writing process. That time never seemed to come, so our first acknowledgements are to Richard Chang and his many talented associates for moving this process along.

We taught ourselves this career development content through our own career and life experiences, by reading a wide variety of business, psychological, financial planning, and career books, and through our partnership of many years with Dr Ann Coil, a creative and talented program developer and writer.

Our *real* teachers, though, were the thousands of clients who attended our workshops and visited our offices with their career challenges and dilemmas. Just when we thought we had heard it all, we would meet someone who had a new and unique story and had the courage and desire to learn something new about themselves and the world of work.

In addition, we would like to thank the many organizations who allowed us to come into their environments to assist in making their specific situation a win-win for everyone involved.

Last, but not least, thanks to Steve and Dennis for their unfailing support of us and the work that we do.

Additional Credits

Edited by Ruth Stingley
Reviewed by Denise Jeffrey
Graphic Layout by Christina Slater
Cover Design by John Odam Design Associates

Preface

Today we are faced with constant changes and increasing challenges that affect our personal and professional lives. Depending on how we address these changes and challenges, they can either be obstacles to growth or opportunities for advancement.

The advantage will belong to those with a commitment to continuous and advantageous learning. The goal of the Publications Division of Richard Chang Associates, Inc. is to provide individuals and organizations with a variety of practical and innovative resources for continuous learning and measurable improvement results.

It is with this goal in mind that we bring you the *Personal Growth and Development Collection*. These books provide realistic and proven advice, techniques, and tools – on a wide range of subjects – to build performance capabilities and achieve lasting results in your personal and professional life.

We hope that once you've had an opportunity to benefit from the *Personal Growth and Development Collection*, and any of the publications available in our *Practical Guidebook Collection*, you will share your thoughts and suggestions with us. We've included a brief Evaluation and Feedback Form at the end of the book that you can fax or send to us.

With your feedback, we can continuously improve the resources we are providing through the Publications Division of Richard Chang Associates, Inc.

Wishing you successful reading,

Richard Y. Chang
President and CEO
Richard Chang Associates, Inc.

Contents

CHAPTER ONE

The Keys to Unlocking Your Career Potential Are Within Reach

Key points

 Knowing yourself is the only way you can unlock the door to your career potential.

 Most people aren't in touch with their true desires, skills, and attitudes toward work.

 Giant leaps aren't the only way to make career changes; you also can take small steps.

 Knowing yourself frees you from the shackles of wrong career decisions.

Suppose someone walked up to you and asked, 'Are you happy doing what you're doing?' How would you answer? Yes? No? It depends? Could you actually specify what would make you happy? Few people can. Certainly, many of us think we know what type of job or situation would make and keep us thrilled about waking up on Monday morning, but do we really?

• Caroline Roshman followed a traditional route – university directly after secondary school, a teaching degree, and five years of teaching in a primary school before marriage and kids. When her children started school, she was ready to re-enter the work world. But now teaching in a primary school no longer holds the same appeal.

- As a child, Jeff Dyer had wanted to be a fireman, to the extent that his parents even built a fire pole in his bedroom. As a teenager, Jeff made extra money at restaurant jobs, first as a dishwasher, then a porter, then a waiter. Jeff stayed in the restaurant business after secondary school, pursuing a career as a manager. Now in his mid-thirties, Jeff wonders if life would have been better in the fire brigade.

- Rebeccah Moriah is a single mum who works extremely hard as a secretary at an insurance company by day and as a telesales person at night. Both jobs pay the bills, but Rebeccah feels that she is working below her ability. 'Why am I not given the chance to move up?' she wonders.

If you were extremely satisfied with your work at present, you wouldn't have picked up this book. It wouldn't have intrigued you. Perhaps your attitude towards work more closely emulates that of Caroline, Jeff, or Rebeccah in the preceding examples. Work isn't quite what you had imagined; you wish you could get more out of your career – more money, more challenge, more joy, more recognition. The list could go on. Or maybe what's lacking can't be found in the career you chose. You'd like to start again in a totally different career, but you can't quite put your finger on what would fulfil your work desires.

'I always suspected the Partners' Lounge looked like this.'

How do you find the keys?

We hate to break it to you, but we can't tell you which road to take on the path to career happiness, and anybody who professes to have a crystal career ball shouldn't be trusted. Why? Because only you can truly tell what interests you, how developed your skills are, and which of your needs must be fulfilled. You alone can discover the keys to unlocking your career potential. In our career consulting business, we have helped many individuals discover career happiness, but it didn't happen until they delved within themselves to uncover their true wants and desires. We provided direction and company, but they still had to walk down the path.

Once you know yourself, you will have the keys to unlocking your career potential. Analysing yourself will provide you with a career checklist, much like a checklist you have when you buy a house or a car, or when you choose a university. It lists your priorities and simultaneously keeps you grounded in reality. You may wish to attend a particular university, but your A level grades direct you elsewhere, so you look closely at your other priorities.

Most people don't create their own checklist. They go about the process backwards, kissing a multitude of frogs before they discover what Prince Charming looks like. It's much more clever to decipher what you want and then work out how to get the most items on your checklist. You want to take the maximum amount of guesswork out of the process, so that you can achieve success early on.

You need to know yourself

You know you best. What you need to distance yourself from are the societal pressures and the people who seem to know better than you what you should be doing. It doesn't matter what your boss, your mum, your friend, your husband, your wife, your kids, or anyone else thinks about your situation. You are the number-one expert on yourself, the only one with a direct line to your desires.

You cannot begin to look for a new career or explore the possibilities within your present career until you analyse who you are and what you want. It's not a test to see if you have fulfilled your parents' wishes or society's expectations or whether you chose the same occupation as a friend. You are not a failure if you need to re-examine and remake many of your early-life decisions. Original decisions do not need to cement your career pattern for life.

Case Study

Richard Dylan, one of our clients, came from a wealthy family; he earned the prerequisite undergraduate degree in business and continued on to law school. However, he realized he did not want to be a lawyer, so he moved to London and became a stockbroker. But Richard had always wanted to tinker around and work with his hands. When he finally listened to himself and his desires, he left the high pressure of the finance world and made a business out of buying and refurbishing antique motorcycles. His original career decision was to follow his parents' wishes, but it was not the desire of his heart.

> *Trust in yourself. Your perceptions are often far more accurate than you are willing to believe.*
>
> Claudia Black

Why aren't you in touch with yourself?

We take other people's word for too many things. From our parents to our teachers to our employers, we have learned what we can and cannot do. We are feedback-oriented; if that feedback is negative, we take it to heart. If it's positive, we bask in pleasure for a moment, then assume that everyone else could do just as well.

Another reason for being out-of-touch with our desires and our abilities is that we are afraid of listening to ourselves. We are afraid of what it means to the other people in our lives, because it means major change for everybody. Some people intuitively know they want to be doing something else, but they fear the ramifications.

How do you find out about yourself?

Case Study

Renee Brown came to us after taking a career test at the university where she was studying for a BA in Industrial Psychology. She took what amounted to two-days' worth of tests at the career centre, answering every question known to man, and it came up with only one career choice for her – managing a convalescent home. The snag? She disliked working with older people, especially older people who were sick.

Wouldn't it be wonderful to take a test to discover what you should do for the rest of your life? Such tests exist, and some people do take them; they carefully answer the test questions, and a computer spits out the previously-elusive answer. What is wrong with this picture? The tests are so limited, and the answers often so nonsensical, it's not worth your time or your money. And if you do abide by the answer given you, it could very well be destructive.

Such a career test can look only at limited parts of you. After supposedly analysing your background, wants, and abilities, it comes up with laundry lists of old careers. One woman took a career test and was shocked by the response she received. For some reason, the computer must have been stuck on *w*, because it told her she could be a *wart remover* or a *worm grower*.

It's not that formal personality testing is not useful. It's just that personality testing is only one piece of the career puzzle, and that piece may not even fit. A woman we know who has a Ph.D. scored as high as you can score on *petrol station attendant*.

We believe in the value of multi-faceted testing, whereby you analyse more than just your personality to arrive at a career you not only could live with, but also thrive on. This testing relies on both rational and emotional responses. Analysing yourself will provide you with a checklist of important considerations, not a job title that has little to do with your true interests.

Your checklist will change. What you want when you're twenty is not necessarily what's important to you at thirty, forty, or fifty. So this process isn't just a one-time test; it's a learning experience you will come back to time and time again to determine what you should be doing, given your desires and your situation. For example, your preference for working with people tends not to change over time, while your need for money often does.

> *What lies behind us and what lies before us are tiny matters, compared to what lies within us.*
>
> Ralph Waldo Emerson

Do you have to use your potential when you discover it?

Absolutely not. It is up to you. A main reason why people don't want to uncover their potential is for fear of having to change what they're currently doing – which is a fear of the unknown. You may be fearful of making a major change in your life. But you don't have to, for example, leave your accountants job today to become a circus performer tomorrow, just because that's what you've discovered. Many people take small steps towards their potential, steps that don't turn their lives upside-down.

Case Study

Victoria Hick, a single parent with a medical degree and a job in banking, came to us for advice. She had two kids, a mortgage, and was in her late thirties. 'I have always wanted to be a medical doctor,' she told us. 'But don't you dare tell me to go back to school. I have kids to support and a lifestyle that won't allow it.' What she ended up doing was finding a job in regulatory affairs for a pharmaceutical company. She is the communicator between the doctors and the public. She answers inquiries from customers, writes letters to the doctors, and solves problems for customers. She gets to use all the skills she already has in the medical environment she loves, without going back to school.

When we evaluated our first two years as career counsellors (*we have now been in the business for over fifteen years*), we thought our programme was a failure, because few people made major career changes. But we have learned that not everyone makes an immediate, giant leap from one career to another. Some people slowly work towards the change, following their own time lines according to their own comfort levels. Others make smaller, less discernible changes within the same career or organization. The path you choose is totally individual.

What will knowing yourself allow you to do?

Case Study

John Reed studied biology at university and was headed towards becoming a dentist like his brother, because he was very attracted to his brother's lifestyle. We suggested that he look carefully at that choice in relation to his own skills. We scheduled a four-hour period for John to visit a dentist and observe exactly what a dentist does. 'I know what it's like to be a patient in a dental surgery,' John responded. 'But you don't want to be a patient,' was our reply. 'You want to be a dentist, so you need to see what a dentist does.' John went to the dental surgery and watched as the dentist worked under a tight time schedule in a small, confined space with tiny instruments. The analysis of John's needs revealed that he liked open-ended schedules and chatting with people in a pleasant environment. John couldn't get over how unhappy the patients were, and he discovered that dentists can't converse with patients who have their mouths either wide-open or full of instruments. With this new information, John returned to university and pursued a combination marketing/biology degree. He also started a networking club for those with biology degrees who didn't want to become either a dentist or a doctor. John ended up doing extremely well in pharmaceutical sales.

What will you get out of this book? If you carefully consider each of the areas that determines your career choice, you'll find that you know much more about your skills, your attitudes, and your desires. You will have the keys to unlocking your career potential. The knowledge you gain will build confidence, allow you to recognize opportunities when they are in front of you, help you articulate what you want, and enable you to make a decision or series of decisions that is truly good for you and free of the constraints of societal or peer pressure.

You will have the courage of true conviction when you know what makes yourself tick. You won't feel the tug of what seems best for you, because you'll know what's best. Many individuals mistakenly get into management, because it's the next rung on the ladder of success. They don't stop to consider whether management is truly in their best interests. They don't listen to that inner voice that says, 'You dislike people problems. You can't stand it when people don't do things right or don't do it on time.' They could be totally miserable. Knowing yourself circumvents such problems.

Conversely, we've heard employees remark, 'I'm supposed to have a career, but I've turned it into a job.' They begin to draw boundaries. They no longer take work home in a briefcase, and they feel their work is something they have to do. Such workers are usually better off in another career or a job.

> *To love what you do and feel that it matters, how could anything be more fun?*
>
> Katherine Graham

Case Study

A client of ours who was nearing retirement age worked in information systems for a major food corporation in the process of reducing its work force. He was offered a small, early retirement pension, which afforded him a limited income. His first thought was to immediately pursue another career in information systems, although that wasn't what he really wanted to do. We asked him, 'What makes you happiest? What makes you alive? Where would you like to be?' His response? 'Wimbledon.' He wanted to be a steward there, so he could watch the games. On the weekends, this gentleman also taught flying at a local airport. Combining the two jobs supplemented his retirement income sufficiently, and he was happy in the transition from career to job.

Become more conscious of the choice you have either to work in a job or a career. As corporations load work on people with jobs, the people get resentful. They don't see where they are going, and they have the worst of both worlds – a job with a lot of stress and a lot of hours. They need to air their feelings with the people in charge or get another job.

Conversely, many corporations at any given moment will let you have a career if you start to make the moves that characterize you as a career person. They won't deny it to you. One company we know has a category called *RFM – Ready For Management* that you place yourself in if you feel that you'd like to pursue a career in management. You start to take extra courses and ask to be viewed differently.

> *A successful career requires falling in love many times with your work.*
>
> *Anonymous*

Whatever your decision, at whatever stage of your life, make sure that it's one that fits your needs. Your attitudes towards work and your motivation for work both play a part in why you work as you do. You've begun exploring what you want based on your attitudes and motivation. Next, you'll explore further by determining where you want to work.

Conclusion

If you held the same attitudes towards work and were motivated by the same things as everyone else, you and the rest of the working world would be competing for the same jobs. But, thank goodness, you don't have the same attitudes and aren't motivated by the same things. Certain jobs or careers appeal to you based on what spurs you forward in the world of work. Delving within to uncover why you work as you do moves you ahead in your quest to unlock your career potential.

CHAPTER FOUR

Deciding Where You Belong

Key points

 For some people, environment greatly influences their career decisions; for others, it makes little difference.

 Choosing your ideal work environment involves identifying the particular tangible and intangible factors important to you.

 An environment's intangibles refer to organizational culture – what you learn by observing the workplace and talking to employees after a hard day's work.

Deciding where you belong holds great interest for some people and little interest for others. One of our clients, a human-resource professional, stipulated that she would only be happy working at a hotel or resort. Another client, a computer technician, told us that it didn't matter whether he worked for an aerospace corporation or a flower shop; in a tall, glass building or in a one-room shed; in a formal, multi-level corporation or a loose, informal company, as long as he was able to work with what he loved – computers.

What's it really like to work there?

A work environment is both a tangible set of physical assets and an intangible way of behaving. The tangible set includes such items as arena, industry, and size. The intangible way of behaving refers to organizational culture. If you have a distinct preference for a certain environment, then it is in your best interests to work through this chapter. You may not even realize the extent of your preferences until you've completed the exercises.

What you'll determine is the ideal environment in which you'd like to work, whether you have a job or a career. Your ideal environment might not be much different from the one you're presently in. On the other hand, it could be so thoroughly different that it stimulates you to finish this book so you have your complete career checklist in hand. You may be ready and eager to look elsewhere.

If you are the type of person who really cares little about your work environment, we give you permission to skim over this chapter. At one company, when we commented about the thick layer of dust on the potted plants, the workers looked at us quizzically. 'What plants?' they asked. But while you may not be interested in the physical environment, you may have particular desires concerning size of company or amount of structure. So scan this chapter, if you must, but don't ignore it.

Case Study

Some of our clients are unaware of how the environment they work in can have such a great bearing on their satisfaction levels. One client, an administrative assistant, was unhappy working in a plush office with sumptuous carpet underneath and beautiful art hanging on the walls. Formal business dress and formal communication were the order of the day. 'It's far too quiet and stiff,' she commented. 'I feel like I'm in a morgue. It completely stifles my creativity.' She went to work for a company whose environment was completely different from her previous one. Workers right on up to the chairman were on a first-name basis, laughed a lot, and worked at desks that had seen better days. All employees wore jeans and T-shirts that had the company's logo printed on the front. 'I feel at home here,' she told us. 'I'm able to accomplish a lot and feel good while I'm doing it.' For her, the right environment made all the difference.

Look at your tangible choices

We will first look at which arenas or industries you might be interested in, as well as the size of your chosen organization. You have many choices within these broad parameters, and you may be attracted to multiple environments, but you do need to narrow down the broad list to the choices you can work in.

Arenas

An arena is the largest description within the work environment. It involves the following sectors: business, nonprofit, education, and government. Circle any or all that you are interested in. Cross out with a line any that you prefer not to work in:

- business;
- nonprofit;
- education/academic;
- government.

Case Study

Gayle Stoll, a woman we met at one of our workshops, was a secondary school English teacher who made a career change from education to business. Attracted to the money and prestige of the entertainment industry, she went to work for a major television network, watching all of their shows in order to write promotional lead-ins for them. The environment was glamorous, and the money was good – she made £40,000 a year. However, she wasn't entirely happy in that setting. She thought carefully about one of the comments we made during our workshop – 'The clues to your future are in your past' – and she started digging up old pictures. She discovered one that revealed her and other neighbourhood children picketing for equal pocket money. Not long after, she went to work for a trade union in public relations and now is extremely content. She travelled from the education arena to business to nonprofit before finally finding her niche.

Industries

Once you've chosen your arena, you need to look at the type of industries you are attracted to. Beside each industry listed, write down the first thought that comes to mind. It might be as generic as *exciting* or as specific as an actual company that the industry brings to mind. Then, circle any of the industries that you are strongly interested in or attracted to. Cross out with a line any that you wish to avoid.

_____Aesthetic, Cultural

_____Biomedical or Biotechnical

_____Business/Corporate

_____Computer

_____Design

_____Entertainment/Media/ Broadcasting

_____Fashion/Image

_____Financial

_____Governmental

_____Healthcare/Nutrition/Fitness

_____Hospital/Medical

_____Hotel/Leisure/Recreation

_____High Technology

_____Food

_____Educational

——Political

——Estate Agency/Development

——Construction

——Retail

——Restaurant

——Telecommunications

——Consumer Goods

——Textile

——Manufacturing

——Sports/Leisure

——Travel/Transportation

——Utilities/Energy

——Consulting

——Computer Graphics

——Home-based Business

——Small Business/Franchise

Your response to both this activity and the one concerning arenas is emotional, based on whether or not you like the industries or arenas listed. It's a starting point meant to trigger ideas. Look at the industries and arenas you circled. Did you circle them because of actual experiences you had or because of perceptions about the industry or arena? Maybe an uncle owned a franchise and made a lot of money. His success story appeals to you. But would you *really enjoy* that opportunity?

Likewise, question yourself concerning the industries and arenas you either crossed out or didn't circle. One of our clients neither circled nor crossed out the academic arena. She didn't dislike it; she thought you needed a great deal of post-graduate training to succeed in that arena. She ended up working as a public-relations person for a small community college, and she enjoys it immensely.

Size

The size of the organization you work for is also critical to some people. Do you desire a small, young organization where you can play many roles and have an impact on the direction and development of a group? Or do you prefer a larger, older organization that has direction, stability, history, and prestige? Such an organization also can provide you with many avenues of growth simply because of size.

Tick which size of an organization you prefer.

———Small: 1–99 employees

———Medium: 100–500 employees

———Large: 500+ employees

Don't overlook the intangibles

Choosing arenas, industries, and size are the tangibles within a work environment. Once you've chosen them, you're ready to look at the intangibles – the organizational culture that dictates how those in the organization behave. This is not information you'll find in the annual report. You would have to observe it in the corridors and the canteen and hang around in the car park as the employees talk about their day.

What you will discover in determining an organization's culture is both the formal structure of the organization and the informal norms and values. Think about what environment you'd like in terms of how the people behave, communicate, look, and work together. Do you prefer an environment that is tightly structured and has a formal chain of command, or would you function better in a looser, more entrepreneurial environment?

Would you be inclined to choose an environment where employees dress more formally and business-like, or one where workers follow an informal dress code? Answering questions like these puts you in the position of knowing what you want. One of our workshop participants went from a tightly-structured environment to one where no one checked up on anyone, and he couldn't get anything done. 'I was one of the first to be let go,' he told us, 'and now I know not to seek employment in such an environment.'

Which do you prefer?

For some individuals, a small company cuts off their circulation. For others, a large one is too impersonal. Find a size that fits you.
                                                                    Keith Stringfellow

To get in touch with your preference for a particular organizational culture, look at the following 11 intangible characteristics of an organization, and place yourself where you fit best on each continuum. Mark your point of preference with an X.

1. Interaction based on a formal   Informal interaction with everyone
    position – or title – basis   regardless of rank or title
    Expect to give: **Expect to give:**
    Due respect for position and formal title   According to individual
    Expect to get: personality and needs
    Ignored at lower levels   **Expect to get:**
                                                            Talked to

    ├──────────┼──────────┼──────────┼──────────┤
    1   2   3   4   5

2. Highly traditional   Loosely-structured and
    chain-of-command   free-flowing
    Expect to give: **Expect to give:**
    Instructions to subordinates   Instructions to everyone,
    Expect to get: regardless of rank or title
    Directions from above, with minimal feedback   **Expect to get:**
    for those at lower levels   Instructions from everyone

    ├──────────┼──────────┼──────────┼──────────┤
    1   2   3   4   5

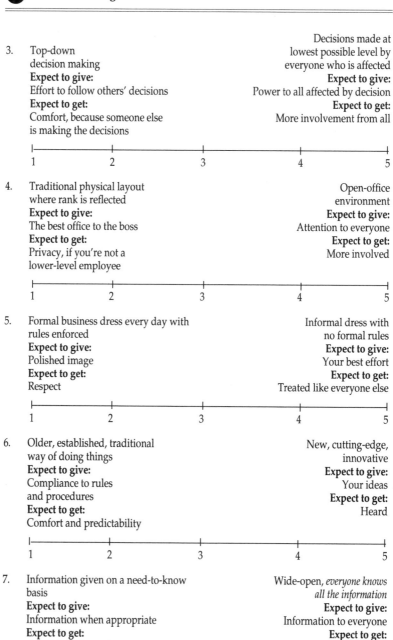

3. Top-down decision making
Expect to give:
Effort to follow others' decisions
Expect to get:
Comfort, because someone else is making the decisions

Decisions made at lowest possible level by everyone who is affected
Expect to give:
Power to all affected by decision
Expect to get:
More involvement from all

|———————————+———————————+———————————+———————————|
1   2   3   4   5

4. Traditional physical layout where rank is reflected
Expect to give:
The best office to the boss
Expect to get:
Privacy, if you're not a lower-level employee

Open-office environment
Expect to give:
Attention to everyone
Expect to get:
More involved

|———————————+———————————+———————————+———————————|
1   2   3   4   5

5. Formal business dress every day with rules enforced
Expect to give:
Polished image
Expect to get:
Respect

Informal dress with no formal rules
Expect to give:
Your best effort
Expect to get:
Treated like everyone else

|———————————+———————————+———————————+———————————|
1   2   3   4   5

6. Older, established, traditional way of doing things
Expect to give:
Compliance to rules and procedures
Expect to get:
Comfort and predictability

New, cutting-edge, innovative
Expect to give:
Your ideas
Expect to get:
Heard

|———————————+———————————+———————————+———————————|
1   2   3   4   5

7. Information given on a need-to-know basis
Expect to give:
Information when appropriate
Expect to get:
Asked for information

Wide-open, *everyone knows all the information*
Expect to give:
Information to everyone
Expect to get:
Lots of questions

|———————————+———————————+———————————+———————————|
1   2   3   4   5

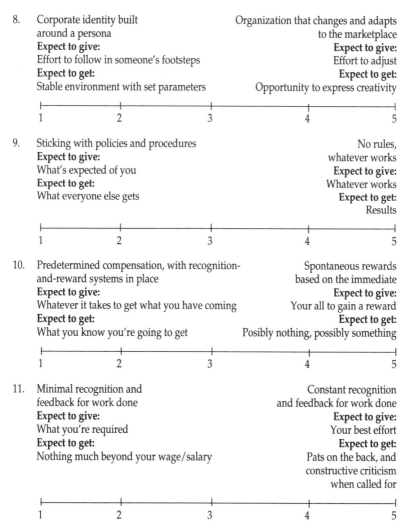

8. Corporate identity built
   around a persona
   Expect to give:
   Effort to follow in someone's footsteps
   Expect to get:
   Stable environment with set parameters

   Organization that changes and adapts
   to the marketplace
   Expect to give:
   Effort to adjust
   Expect to get:
   Opportunity to express creativity

   ```
   |——————————|——————————|——————————|——————————|
   1          2          3          4          5
   ```

9. Sticking with policies and procedures
   Expect to give:
   What's expected of you
   Expect to get:
   What everyone else gets

   No rules,
   whatever works
   Expect to give:
   Whatever works
   Expect to get:
   Results

   ```
   |——————————|——————————|——————————|——————————|
   1          2          3          4          5
   ```

10. Predetermined compensation, with recognition-
    and-reward systems in place
    Expect to give:
    Whatever it takes to get what you have coming
    Expect to get:
    What you know you're going to get

    Spontaneous rewards
    based on the immediate
    Expect to give:
    Your all to gain a reward
    Expect to get:
    Posibly nothing, possibly something

    ```
    |——————————|——————————|——————————|——————————|
    1          2          3          4          5
    ```

11. Minimal recognition and
    feedback for work done
    Expect to give:
    What you're required
    Expect to get:
    Nothing much beyond your wage/salary

    Constant recognition
    and feedback for work done
    Expect to give:
    Your best effort
    Expect to get:
    Pats on the back, and
    constructive criticism
    when called for

    ```
    |——————————|——————————|——————————|——————————|
    1          2          3          4          5
    ```

Do you now have a feel for the type of environment you prefer? Sometimes it involves trying out a new or different environment; we have had clients go kicking and screaming into a new environment and end up loving it. Others intuitively know what they want and what they don't want. These people should not be *stuck* where they don't want to be. It just won't work.

Describe your ideal environment. Consider both the tangible and intangible factors.

When people have an intense desire to work in a particular environment, it's easy to satisfy them. They are so sure they want to work in a shopping centre or in a hospital, it's just a matter of finding appropriate employment within that environment. Since ideal work must still match one's interest and skills, the search often involves exploring both traditional and nontraditional work within the preferred environment.

For example, if you desire to work in a shopping centre, you could sell clothes in a clothes shop, park cars, work in a restaurant, or manage a shop. If those don't appeal to you, you might consider tenant relations, marketing, or community relations, all nontraditional jobs related to a shopping centre. If you'd rather not be a doctor, nurse, physiotherapist, or a porter, but you really want to work in a hospital, expand your horizons. Maybe you'd do well in patient relations, business development, or hospital administration.

> *If you know where you want to work, you only need directions for getting there.*
>
> *Anonymous*

Case Study

Jack Browning, one of our clients who was an accountant, expressed a great deal of interest in motorcycles. He liked to be around them so much, he went to work for a major motorcycle distributor. Half of the employees rode motorcycles to work, including some of the secretaries. A real motorcycle was on display in the lobby, the walls were covered with pictures of motorcycles, and at lunch time, all the employees talked about ...? You guessed it – motorcycles! Jack could have been an accountant anywhere, but he chose an environment that really interested him, and it increased his satisfaction.

If a particular environment interests you, you will have a good starting point from which to direct your career inquiries. If you don't have much of an opinion one way or the other, your pool of possibilities will be much larger. It's unquestionably an individual choice that leads to a clearer definition of your ideal career.

Conclusion

Few people are absolutely certain which environment they want to work in. It's easy to direct those people on a career path. On the other end of the spectrum are those who care little about which environment they are placed in. They also number in the minority; we direct them towards the other keys to unlocking their career potential. Most people fall somewhere in the middle, sure of some factors and oblivious about others.

Deciding where you belong entails researching both the tangible and the intangible factors concerning work environment. Once you have settled on your choices, you can concentrate on the other keys, secure in the fact that you're getting closer to creating your career checklist.

Knowing Who or What to Work With

Are you into people, data, or things? You would think that people would know intuitively with what or whom they prefer to work, but we've found that it's often the last thing on their minds. We've seen a number of data people in customer-service positions. They are terribly unhappy, but not sure why. Such a mismatch – between what or who you want to work with and the reality of the position you're in – usually causes what we call *career pain*. The degree of your career pain can result in symptoms as irritating as a dull headache or as tormenting as an old knee injury.

Are you suffering from career pain?

If you absolutely love your job, you most likely fit well in your position. But if you got laid off tomorrow, would you be able to describe exactly what type of job would fit your preference for things, data, or people? Most people cannot. And many people are not totally happy in their current positions (ie, *they're suffering from some degree of career pain*), because perhaps they favour working with people while their work requires fixing things or playing with data. Or they would rather be by themselves, but they ended up in a career that involves a great deal of people contact.

Take a look at the following assessment. For each of the ten statements, tick yes or no.

People, data, things – which am I into?

Yes___ No ___ 1. I need to leave my work space often to get my *people fix* during the day.

Yes___ No ___ 2. I love to be immersed in data.

Yes___ No ___ 3. I've been fixing and tinkering with things since childhood.

Yes___ No ___ 4. Interaction with people often leaves me energized.

Yes___ No ___ 5. I'd rather gather the data and write the report than deliver the information to people.

Yes___No ___ 6. I get so caught up in working with data that I forget to eat.

Yes___ No ___ 7. I love working with my hands.

Yes___ No ___ 8. I feel challenged by working with groups of people.

Yes___ No ___ 9. I would be very happy to work all day long by myself.

Yes___ No___ 10. I'm the first one to volunteer to head a committee or organize a meeting.

Scoring key

People person: Answers yes to numbers 1, 4, 8, and 10
Data person: Answers yes to numbers 2, 5, 6, and 9
Things person: Answers yes to numbers 3, 7, and 9

To further test your preferences and to see whether your current job fits your ideal in terms of who or what you work with, look at the following pie charts. Given an enjoyable eight-hour work day, what portion of your time would you like to spend working with data, what amount of time would you choose to spend working with people, and how much time would you allot for working with things? Assume that you are working with people, data, and things that you like in the way you would like. Divide Pie A, your Ideal Work Day, into three sections to represent the three different possibilities and label each.

Next, look at Pie B, your Current Work Day. Also divide this pie into three separate sections – data, people, or things, but do so according to a typical work day at your current job. Again, label each section.

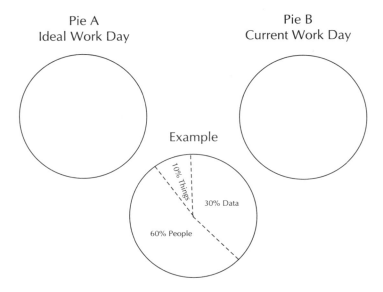

Pie A
Ideal Work Day

Pie B
Current Work Day

Example

10% Things

30% Data

60% People

Does your ideal work-day pie reflect the preferences you stated in the assessment? In other words, if your assessment revealed that you prefer data, did you cut a huge slice for data in your ideal work-day pie? Also look at the similarities or differences between your ideal and your current work-day pies. Are they identical or is there a discrepancy between the two?

If there is a discrepancy and you're suffering career pain, think about how you could alleviate it. Is it possible to expand or limit your *people*, *data*, or *things* time to match your preferences? Or might a new position in a different organization be better? If a career change isn't on the cards, you can re-balance your life by emphasizing your preferences in your personal life. Introverts who are in people-oriented jobs often spend their weekends and vacations alone. And we've counselled extroverted clients who work in jobs with minimal people contact to do the opposite. They might join a golf club or organize the PTA.

Case Study

Rob Matthews, a client of ours, had a degree, but he didn't know what he wanted to do. He happened upon the construction business, and he took a job in construction, which was basically a 'things' job. While Rob was good with his hands, it wasn't satisfying to him. Eventually, he was promoted to a management position in the construction business, but he didn't enjoy managing people either. When we worked with him on assessing his preferences, we discovered that he liked a perfect combination of data, people, and things, each taking an equal third of his ideal work-day pie. He found a position within the financial world, where his work day is split equally between clients, the data they provide him with, and working on his computer. He could make more money if he had more clients, but he would never do that, because it would upset his preferred balance.

Realizing that a huge rift exists between your desires and reality can be incredibly unsettling. Try to build a bridge while you can still see the other side.

Denna Tredo

What's behind your balance (or lack thereof)?

What exactly does a data person enjoy doing? How about a people person, or a things person? Each style of work involves enjoyment of different types of tasks.

People person

A people person enjoys spending time in meaningful interaction with people. This interaction may involve meeting, directing or being directed, brainstorming, teaching, planning, and giving and getting feedback. It can take place one-to-one, in small or large groups, or in teams. Most people cannot handle spending all of their time with people, because constant interaction is energy draining.

Data person

A data person thrives on working with numbers, facts, general information, ideas and concepts, principles and theories, or some combination of these. Don't interpret working with data as only library research. You deal with data when you gather information from people face-to-face or by phone; when you plan and organize projects; or when you review or read magazines, newspapers, and books.

Things person

A things person finds satisfaction in arranging, designing, manipulating, operating, or fixing things. Things can include art objects, communication tools, machinery, equipment, craft materials, plants, and so on. Some people enjoy working with things for leisure and recreation, but prefer not to add things to their *work load*.

For the most part, your enjoyment of or preference for working with people, data, or things changes little. It derives from your personality, and you were born with it. If you've always desired to work with people, you won't be transformed into a hermit any time soon. You can make small or subtle changes, but we've only seen people make major changes in circumstances where they've been out of balance for so long that they head to the other extreme. However, such a switch rarely lasts.

If an organization attempts to change your balance when you've been happy with it, it will be very upsetting. One of our clients loved working with computers. His boss picked up on his knowledge and expertise and decided he'd be great in sales. When the company offered him a big raise to transfer into sales, we counselled him not to take it. He wasn't a people person and would have been extremely unhappy in sales.

The world of work doesn't necessarily understand the importance of maintaining your preferred balance. And, truthfully, most people don't either. You may be offered promotions or raises to take a position that doesn't fit your style of work. People can work out of their style to some degree, but not without consequences. So knowing your preferences and sticking with them is the best bet for you.

The truth about people persons

We'd be rich if we had a penny for everyone who came to us for career counselling and said, 'I don't know what I want to do, but I do want to work with people.' That's nowhere near a definitive answer. Granted, it's a starting point, but you need to delve much further to come up with an idea of what type of career would match your interests. It's helpful to know you want to work with people; and, in the pie exercise, you also had to determine how much of your work day you wanted to spend with people. But we can't solve your career dilemma on the basis of that information alone. You also need to figure out who you want to work with and in what way you want to work with them.

Who are they?

You're certain you want to work with people for at least one portion of your work day. But exactly what type of people do you want to work with? We could suggest that you work with senior citizens or pregnant women, but you might have no interest in either of those groups. Unless you specify your interests, you won't be much further ahead in formulating your career checklist.

> *You may like working with people, but do people like working with you?*
>
> *Anonymous*

Case Study

We counselled a teacher, Roberta Henderson, who had one of the most extroverted personalities we had ever seen. She told us, 'I want to get out of teaching.' When she completed her ideal work-day pie, we noticed that she had reduced the amount of time she wanted to spend with people. 'In teaching, people contact is about 90 percent of the pie,' she said. 'I don't think I can tolerate any more than 30 or 40 percent of people contact.' But Roberta's personality was so people-oriented, she would not be happy with such a reduction. 'It's "who" you work with that's the problem,' we told her. 'You're not cut out for teaching children. If you would train adults, you'd want the 90 percent people contact.' She did pursue training adults and is extremely satisfied.

Place a check mark by any or all of the following groups of people with whom you would be interested in working.

—— Peers, colleagues
—— Subordinates
—— Upper management
—— Clients/customers
—— Vendors
—— General public
—— Other departments:
　　—— Accounting/finance
　　—— Information systems
　　—— Human resources

—— Sales/marketing
—— Other

Special populations: (*This is a list to begin to jog your thinking*)

—— Small-business owners/Entrepreneurs
—— Children
—— Older adults
—— Women
—— Professional practitioners (*doctors, dentists, etc.*)
—— The general public
—— Handicapped individuals
—— People in poor health
—— Individuals who are looking for fun and entertainment
—— People in need
—— Those with great financial resources
—— Teenagers
—— Minorities
—— Men
—— Other

Case Study

Harry Steinman, one of our clients who was a former teacher, took a position in pharmaceutical sales, selling prescription drugs to doctors. He came to us because he found himself sitting in car parks, faking his call reports. 'I made the wrong decision,' he said. 'I should not be in sales.' The results of his assessment revealed that he had made the right decision. What was wrong was his 'who'. We asked Harry if he liked doctors, and he said, 'No'. 'Well,' we suggested, 'you should consider selling products to someone other than doctors.' Harry is now selling medical-benefit packages to entrepreneurs in small- to medium-sized companies, and he's as happy as can be, because he enjoys working with business owners.

Maybe your career is a nightmare, not because of the amount of people contact but who you are in contact with. For example, we dealt with the employees of a customer-service department who were being laid off. Half the people we counselled revealed that they were *people* persons and knew to look for another customer-service position. The other half of the department should never have been in a customer-service job in the first place. They were either extremely data-oriented people who happened upon a customer-service position or they didn't enjoy working with the *who* in their job – the general public. They needed to find positions that involved working with specific groups they enjoyed.

In what way?

It's not just the *who* you have to identify; you also have to figure out *how* you want to work with them. You may enjoy working with senior citizens in an entertainment or liaison role, but you'd rather not lead nor manage them. The ways in which you interact with people can be very different, and you will have distinct preferences about which roles you'd like to play.

> *A role shouldn't be a personality you put on when you get to work. It should be a natural extension of your soul.*
>
> Ruth Gurney

Some ways of interacting will be more satisfying and successful for you than others, depending on your personality and your philosophy about human behaviour and motivation. These ways of interacting are referred to as the roles you play with people in a work situation. Sometimes these ways of interaction, or roles, will be formalized in a job title, like manager or teacher, but there are many informal roles we play, such as liaison or negotiator. You're most happy when you're allowed or encouraged to play the roles you like.

The following ten roles are common ones that people play in work situations: counsellor, resourcer, entertainer, manager, expert/consultant, leader, liaison, negotiator/mediator, educator/teacher, and marketer/promoter. Think about which ones you do play, which you prefer to play, and which ones you play but don't enjoy.

Counsellor

The counsellor believes that the whole person, including feelings and emotions is important. The counsellor sees him or herself as a facilitator to help people get in touch with their inner selves, feelings, and needs. The counsellor can tolerate close, more intense relationships with people and is not put off by the less positive, less upbeat, and more depressing side of human nature. Counsellors feel rewarded by solving people's problems at a personal and emotional level. Teachers, psychologists, social workers, and ministers of religion are obvious career examples of the counselling role. Many people, however, who haven't obtained a credential or license can play an effective, informal, and natural role of counsellor with colleagues.

Resourcer

The resourcer believes that people will be happier and more productive when they have access to the information they need. The resourcer believes that there is power in knowledge and likes to help people solve problems by helping them gain access to information, people, and other resources. Resourcers like to help people solve problems, but at a less personal, more objective level than the counsellor. A resource librarian or computer information manager are clear career examples of the resourcer role, as is anyone in any researching role.

Entertainer

An entertainer is not necessarily a stand-up comedian. The entertainer believes that there is much to be optimistic about in life and usually identifies positive qualities in people. The entertainer believes that people will be happiest and most productive if they can operate in an efficient, effective, positive environment that brings out their best. Entertainers delight in setting up events and environments where people can enjoy themselves and work productively. An obvious entertainer role is played by people in travel, meeting-and-events planning, and leisure and recreation.

Manager

The manager believes that people will be more productive and happy, and the world will work more efficiently, if there is a scheme, a plan, and someone – mainly himself or herself – to construct and oversee this plan. The manager derives satisfaction from being able to elicit good work from others (*such as creating things, organizing, selling, and implementing*). However, managers do not feel compelled to do more work themselves. What they enjoy is to direct, influence, and control others, and to have an impact on the direction and development of a unit, group, or organization. The manager can tolerate supervising, monitoring, evaluating, and admonishing.

Expert/Consultant

The expert/consultant enjoys having, and being perceived as having, special knowledge, expertise, or technical competence in a certain area. The expert/consultant enjoys serving and responding to people by solving a problem or fulfilling a need through the use of his or her particular expertise. Like the resourcer, the expert/consultant prefers to work at a less personal level than the counsellor. However, the expert/consultant views him or herself as a specialist with more in-depth, specific knowledge than the resourcer, who is more of a generalist.

Leader

A leader believes that people need direction, cohesiveness, and a common motivation if they are to work together. A leader is someone who keeps a group moving towards common goals. A leader can motivate; will establish and maintain lines of communication; and is good at establishing rapport, making people feel comfortable, and welcoming individuals into a group. A leader is not always talkative and outgoing, although many are. There are many quiet, covert leaders – people who draw others to them naturally and easily because of their knowledge, resources, and interpersonal skills. All managers should be leaders, but not all leaders necessarily need to be managers.

Liaison

The liaison believes that people in groups will operate more effectively if there is open and free-flowing communication. So the liaison is the communication bridge between two people, two groups, or two organizations. The liaison is able to balance loyalties and remain objective, can see both sides of the situation, and can translate ideas clearly. Community relations is a liaison position in which an individual represents a company or organization to the community and carries the community's interests and issues back to the company.

Negotiator

Negotiators, like liaisons, are communicators between people and groups. A negotiator, however, derives satisfaction from communicating in situations that involve conflict, dissension, or disagreements that must be resolved. The negotiator is skilled in helping two opposing sides arrive at consensus and compromise, and thrives on the challenge to establish communication and arrive at solutions in pressured and sensitive situations. Lobbyists, lawyers, labour negotiators, and mediators are obvious career examples of the negotiator role.

Educator/Teacher

One doesn't have to be a trained teacher to play an educator role. The educator, like the resourcer, believes that knowledge is important, but goes beyond to help people also develop skills and change attitudes. Teachers have a natural ability to describe things clearly, see the sequence of things (*including information*), and know how to approach and instruct different people in different and most appropriate ways. Teachers are patient and can put themselves in the place of the person who needs to start slowly at the beginning.

Marketer/Promoter

The marketer/promoter believes that people will be happy if they are persuaded and moved to action. Marketers gain satisfaction from getting behind a cause, person, thing, or activity and motivating others to 'buy in.' They are enthusiastic, although not always obviously so, and can get others to catch on to the enthusiasm and join the bandwagon. Sales people are obvious marketers and promoters, but so is the person who does fund-raising for a local charitable group, or the person in the office who can convince everyone to come to the company outing or to agree to the new personnel policy.

Complete the following 'Annual Meeting' exercise that's designed to help you determine which roles you enjoy playing in a work situation.

How to work with people – annual meeting

A committee has been assembled to put together your company's annual meeting to *team build* and inform employees on new developments and products. What do you want to do? Circle the roles you would enjoy playing. Cross out those you prefer not to play.

Counsellor

Likes personal relationships; enjoys counselling and advising people on committee who need help or need to feel more included.

Resourcer

Good at and enjoys searching out/locating needed equipment, resources, and information to put on the event.

Entertainer

Focuses on creating a comfortable and inviting environment where everyone will feel welcome and included.

Leader

Motivates and inspires committee and employees towards goal of having an enjoyable and productive meeting. Communicates goal to others.

Liaison

Naturally links and connects individuals and departments so all know what is going on and understand each other's part.

Negotiator/Mediator

Not averse to negotiating between departments/managers with differing views/needs; enjoys negotiating for employees' time off and to acquire an appropriate budget to plan the event.

Manager

Wants to manage and direct activities of the committee and/or the whole event.

Educator/Trainer

Responsible for making a presentation that informs and enlightens people about new products, programmes, and how to use them, etc.

Expert/Consultant

Likes being called on for knowledge and expertise to make a contribution or to solve a problem.

Marketer/Promoter

Formally or informally gets people to buy in to attending and getting involved in the event.

Which roles do you play in your current job? Are they the same as the ones you identified in the *Annual Meeting* exercise? Sometimes we encourage clients to get rid of a role they don't enjoy. For example, many people are managers and would rather just be leaders. Other clients we ask to consider formalizing a role by getting a certificate or a degree; still others might need to transfer to a different department within their present organization. Having the opportunity and the recognition for playing your preferred roles has a lot to do with your career satisfaction and productivity.

Getting yourself re-balanced

Balance is essential. You can't succeed while teetering on the brink of 'career dislike'.

Anonymous

So you find yourself out-of-balance. You'd rather spend more time working on things, or you're not working with the type of people you would like to. Or it could be that you're not allowed to play the roles you enjoy. What can you do to remedy the situation, to alleviate your career pain?

This is one of the aspects of your career that you have more control over. You can manoeuvre minor changes within an organization or your personal life, and you can also make major changes if need be.

Minor changes

It's not too difficult to tweak your job ever so slightly or make a small change in your personal life to make you more satisfied with what or whom you work. Consider the following suggestions if you're interested in making minor changes:

- To increase your people contact, volunteer at work to participate on a committee or team.

- Talk to your boss about changing a task in your job description that you dislike.

- Conversely, talk to your boss about adding tasks that you enjoy.

- Balance your need for people, data, and things by pursuing a hobby or volunteer work that fills your need.

Case Study

One of our clients, Myra Robinson, is vice-president of information systems at a financial institution, which is a heavily data- and things-oriented job. Because she is such an extrovert, on her own time she serves on committees. She is on the Board of Governors at a local school, and she recently formed an advisory committee on women's health issues. Her volunteer work fills her need for people contact; participating in the volunteer work allows her to function well in a data- and things-oriented job.

Major changes

Please think through all major changes carefully. And, of course, any major change should take all five keys into consideration, so you'll need to finish this book before you hand in your resignation or approach your boss. But it is helpful to think about some of the options available to you if you can't be satisfied by making minor changes.

You may need to make a complete change in both your choice of career and the type of people you are working with. But before going to such an extreme, analyse why you are unhappy. Maybe your career is right for you, but you need to change the population of people you work with. Caroline Roshman, the primary school teacher we introduced you to in the first chapter of this book, didn't want to teach infants. She ended up going on to further education, volunteered to teach an evening class of adult students, and discovered she loved it. She toyed with the idea of giving up teaching altogether, but now she's so glad she didn't, because she has found that teaching adults is what really suits her.

Another change you might consider is doing something different with the same people. Jim Markworth, a manager of customer-service representatives at a major utility company, was tired of the long hours and the headaches involved in playing the manager role. He switched over to training the customer service representatives instead of managing them and is much more content.

Checking your balance of people, data, and things in your current position and determining if it fits your preferences is worth your effort. For many, it's a connection they've never before made, one that makes a great deal of sense. And it brings you a step closer to unlocking your career potential.

When you don't enjoy what you do, work becomes more and more like work.

Michelle Herkimer

Conclusion

If you're in a job or position that doesn't match your preferences for working with people, data, and/or things, you know what career pain feels like. The greater the mismatch, the more insistent your pain. But it can be remedied, with either minor changes to your particular job or personal life, or through a major modification of the career roles you play or the population you work with. It's a key that can lead to greater job satisfaction.

'Actually, I'm a waiter. I'm only doing this until I find a restaurant that suits my talents.'

CHAPTER SIX

Looking at What You Bring to the Table

Key points

 Few people really know what skills they possess.

 Knowing your technical, personal, and transferable skills unlocks your career potential by putting you in touch with what you do best and what you prefer to do.

 Once you uncover your preferred skills, you'll know what kind of work fits your abilities.

Some people apply for jobs and are hired for the wrong reasons. They apply for jobs that fit their work experience, degrees, and/or credentials and shy away from jobs that don't. And they often are hired to do work that doesn't suit their skills or that they don't even like, just because they have the required degree or experience. Why? Because most employers don't know which skills are necessary for the jobs they're trying to fill, and most employees can't identify all of the skills they possess.

It's time for a change. Pinpointing your skills will open up doors to new career opportunities. We're willing to wager that you possess more skills than you believe you do, some which you developed outside the work arena and which could land you a job you would enjoy. And we also bet that you may be using some skills in your current job that you're not particularly thrilled about using. Knowing your preferred skills provides you with a plethora of options.

Don't wait for the eulogy

Everyone is aware that they possess skills, and they can identify some of them. 'I'm great on the telephone,' commented one secretary. 'My boss tells me that all the time.' Another participant in one of our workshops, Maurice Selwood, an estate agent, told us he was good at sales. 'I know I am because I'm one of the top sellers, and I receive an award every year. But,' Maurice said and paused to think for a moment, 'I can't really say that I'm good at much else. And while it provides a decent living, selling property is not my favourite activity.'

Unfortunately, like Maurice, most people don't come close to knowing all of the skills they possess. People often skate by for years without touching on everything that they do well, because they know they have some skills and that's sufficient for them. Yet awareness of your skills will help you unlock your career potential.

Why don't you know your skills?

Like Maurice, most people take themselves for granted; they see their skills as things they do so easily, they don't recognize them as valuable. We were able to help Maurice identify a load of skills he was unaware of. He had tremendous problem-solving skills, was great in marketing, and was ahead of many in his ability to communicate ideas clearly to his clients. 'I thought everybody could do those things,' Maurice said. Wrong. Each person has a unique set of skills; your set is not representative of your next-door neighbour's.

> *We habitually use only a small part of the powers we actually possess.*
> *William James*

Another reason why you may not be aware of your skills is because you may not receive enough positive feedback in life. Most people aren't told when they do things well. You probably can recite more things that you can't do than things you can. And you may be more reticent to share what you do well because you don't want to brag or boast.

Case Study

One of our clients, Margaret Trilling, a registered nurse who had been out of the work force for twenty years, came to us for career counselling. We asked her what skills she had, and she replied, 'None'. We investigated further, asking her what she did with her time. It so happened that Margaret's husband was a pilot who was shot down during the Vietnam war, and she helped start the MIA/POW group that eventually grew into a movement. She got together with other wives, and Margaret in particular decided the issue should receive national attention. She researched other major movements to learn about organization, and decided to go to Washington D.C. as an unpaid lobbyist. She was even brought into briefings with Henry Kissinger and Alexander Haig, took a world tour and met with heads of state and the Pope, and ended up in North Vietnam. She now works for her country in an advocacy position, lobbying for low-cost housing. This is our most extreme example of a client being unaware of the valuable skills she possessed.

It's at the end of our lives when people are willing to remember us for what we did well. But why wait for the eulogy? You need to know what you do well now, when you can choose to use those skills in a career that will satisfy you.

'Mavis, it's me. I'm calling from my portable phone. Thanks for the touching eulogy. I should of asked for a raise when I had the chance.'

Why do you need to know your skills?

Knowing your skills can open up a whole new world of opportunities. It can help you:

- make a better career decision in the first place, because you'll have a clearer idea of what work makes you successful and satisfied if you know what you like to do;

- look for creative ways to do your current job and expand it, if possible;

- begin to target other possible job opportunities within your organization or company;

- make intelligent decisions about which courses, seminars, or workshops you need to take to develop new and additional skills;

- begin to build your career path on a solid base of your best or most finely-honed skills;

- gain confidence as you begin the job-search process;

- recognize others' skills so you know who to work with and how to work with them.

There is nothing more powerful nor more exciting than knowing what you do well. Knowing which skills you wish to use is also a big advantage. For example, you may be great at organizing and coordinating details, but if you don't like details, you will feel trapped, restless, and frustrated in work that requires a great deal of attention to detail. If, instead, you prefer to use creative skills to develop new ideas and see the big picture while working on projects, then you will be most happy and satisfied in a work situation that allows you to do just that.

Pinpoint your skills

A skill is defined as *a learned power of doing something competently.* The fact that it is a power implies that it affords you control. The more skills you possess, the more control you can have over your career. Don't get depressed here. When we explain this in our workshops, some of our clients start frowning and dropping their heads. When we ask them why, they respond with, 'But I don't have many skills. How am I ever supposed to get ahead?'

Our response? 'You have many, many more skills than you think you do. Just wait. We're going to let you in on the three kinds of skills, and we'll ask you to identify each of those skills. If you don't list more skills than you thought you possessed, then you can get depressed.' But we guarantee you won't.

The three kinds of skills we describe to our clients are technical, personal, and transferable skills. Everyone possesses all three types of skills, although a few people rely solely on personal and transferable skills.

Technical skills

Technical skills are specialized, job-specific skills that usually require training to learn. Such skills are obvious, measurable, and easy to describe. Typing, computer, accounting, lab research, sewing, engineering, and medical skills are all examples of technical skills. Most technical skills have to be kept up-to-date. Outdated computer or medical skills won't do you much good.

Besides technical skills, people also gather specialized knowledge. Specialized knowledge is a body of knowledge or information that you have accumulated over a period of time by learning about or working in a particular industry. It may be knowledge of labour law, how the legal system works, learning theory, personnel policies, wage and compensation procedures, how the body works, nutrition, etc. This body of knowledge is a marketable commodity, and is as important as the technical skills you possess.

Case Study

Karen Elmwood, a special-needs teacher who attended one of our workshops, recounted an example of how she acquired specialized knowledge that could have led to a new career. At the beginning of the school year, she was given ten children, and none of them were toilet trained. 'I anticipated a very long year,' Karen said. She hired a consultant who specialized in toilet training, and all ten children were trained within four months. The consultant offered Karen a position in her toilet-

training practice, but Karen declined. 'I knew more about toilet train-
ing than I wanted to know,' she said. 'I never thought about it being a
marketable body of knowledge, but it was. I just wasn't interested in
pursuing a career based on it.'

List any technical skills you possess. Put a star (★) by the
skills you would like to continue to use in a work situation.

_____   _____
_____   _____
_____   _____
_____   _____
_____   _____
_____   _____
_____   _____
_____   _____
_____

As with technical skills, you need to determine what knowledge you have and to what degree you want to continue
using it. List your areas of specialized knowledge and put a
star (★) by the knowledge you want to continue to use in a
work situation.

_____   _____
_____   _____
_____   _____
_____   _____
_____   _____

——————————— ———————————

——————————— ———————————

——————————— ———————————

——————————— ———————————

——————————— ———————————

Personal skills

Some people think that skills only refer to specialized or technical abilities. Not so. Personal skills are skills that flow from personality traits and allow a person to adapt to various work roles and work conditions. We refer to personal skills as boy scout and girl guide qualities, such as integrity, perseverance, thoroughness, patience, commitment, and loyalty. They describe what you are like.

Personal skills

Personal skills are traits or qualities that are useful in any career, any lifestyle, and life itself. Put a check (✓) by those personal skills you possess. Put a star (★) by the five (5) that you consider either your *best* or *most important* personal skills.

—— Hard-working
—— Decisive
—— Independent
—— Enthusiastic
—— Self-starting
—— Creative
—— Personable
—— Goal-oriented
—— Energetic
—— Friendly
—— Eager
—— Tenacious
—— Loyal
—— Trustworthy

—— Flexible
—— Fair
—— Helpful
—— Team player
—— Action-oriented
—— Empathetic
—— Forward-thinking
—— Humorous
—— Clever
—— Reliable
—— Punctual
—— Optimistic
—— Cooperative
—— Versatile

—— Quick-to-learn   —— Self-confident
—— Reasonable   —— Diplomatic
—— Thoughtful   —— Generous
—— Organized   —— Good judgement
—— Detail-oriented   —— Poised
—— Honest   —— Self-controlled
—— Meticulous   —— Tactful
—— Open-minded   —— Dependable

Transferable skills

Transferable skills come from all areas of your life, and they never expire. Transferable skills are ones you use every day. They can appear at any age, and they go with you wherever you go. We describe them as a suitcase of valuable commodities that you take with you. You can go from the non-paid world of work into the paid world with this suitcase, from one industry to another, from job to job, or from one department to another.

What are some of these transferable skills? They range from communication, leadership, and management skills to programme development, public relations, and promoting skills. Whether you're in a technical or a non-technical job, you will still use your transferable skills. For example, interpersonal and communication skills are important whether you are a teacher, computer programmer, manager, sales assistant, or doctor.

Case Study

One of our clients developed strong organizational skills as a flight attendant. She had to quickly and efficiently serve customers dinner and cocktails in a short period of time in cramped and sometimes bumpy quarters. She also developed interpersonal skills that she used to soothe upset customers dripping with grapefruit wedges after a bout with turbulence. She took these transferable skills with her when she acquired a job as a manager in human resources.

Transferable skills come from five areas of your life: work, volunteer activities, leisure and recreation, education, and your personal life. When people change careers, we often look at the four non-paid areas of their lives more than the paid area, because it gives us a better indication of what they want to do. Generally, in the non-paid areas of your life, you're choosing to do what you want to do.

Many people develop transferable skills at work through volunteer activities. Teachers who design instructional units on science, history, or language acquire programme development skills. Volunteers who work on local committees to improve traffic safety can develop negotiating and lobbying skills. And in heading committees and volunteer projects, you can develop and refine leadership skills.

Vocational and leisure time also provides opportunities to learn transferable skills. A client who was a constant gatherer of information for trips and hobbies and children's interests is now a personal assistant to an MP. She researches community and political issues.

In addition, you can develop skills through your personal life. Staging weddings, anniversaries, and parties requires a host of skills such as creating a proper environment, making people feel comfortable, being able to initiate conversations, and timing events effectively.

Finally, from the world of training and education, you can develop critical and analytical-thinking skills, writing and communication skills, and research and problem-solving skills. These also are skills you will use in almost every position you take. We develop valuable, transferable skills in all aspects of our life and at all times of our life.

Few people realize just how many transferable skills they have developed over their lifetime. Look at the following list of transferable skills and the tasks that people who exhibit such skills perform. We're sure that this list will help you identify more transferable skills than you thought you possessed.

> *Everyone has skills. You can't make it through life without mastering at least a few skills.*
>
> *Anonymous*

List of transferable skills

Research and information-gathering skills

Tasks: Gathering information formally or informally, in oral or written form; enjoying the challenge of the hunt for information – not just library research, but phoning for it, asking people for it, taking notes at a lecture, pulling a page out of a newspaper or magazine, etc.

Communication skills

Tasks: Conveying information accurately, interestingly, and clearly; includes oral communication with individuals or groups, using writing skills, and public speaking.

Management skills

Tasks: Monitoring and maintaining progress of a project, activity, or organization; balancing individual and organizational needs; budgeting; delegating; hiring and firing; evaluating people and activities; developing and implementing plans to meet goals; working with all levels of people within a group or organization.

Leadership skills

Tasks: Leading people formally or informally; having a goal or vision; communicating that vision to others; motivating people to follow that goal or vision; being a role model; spearheading and organizing activities so others know what to do; always finding yourself *in charge* of things. Every manager should be a leader, but not every leader is a manager.

Interpersonal skills

Tasks: Being acutely aware of human behaviour and motivation and how your actions and language can negatively or positively affect others' actions and reactions; reading people; being sensitive to their needs and points of view; establishing rapport; gaining people's confidence; manoeuvring and refining situations so that interactions between people will be positive and productive; liking and creating harmony.

Organizing and implementing skills

Tasks: Identifying, prioritizing, and coordinating information, activities, resources, time, and people; getting in and doing the job; attending to and following up with details; bringing a project or task to completion; not just *planning* the task, but being willing to get involved in the doing.

Planning and policy-development skills

Tasks: Recognizing and stating a problem, goal, or direction to take; identifying relevant issues; devising a solution or approach; predicting future needs and determining actions to meet those needs; setting out recommendations, procedures, and policies (*strategic planning for an organization or serving on an advisory board*).

Creating and developing skills

Tasks: Conceptualizing new ideas or approaches to improve a situation or solve a problem; being innovative; doing old things in new ways; pulling ideas or information together in new ways; developing systems, approaches, processes, and techniques; changing things so as not to become bored doing routine activities.

Promoting skills

Tasks: Promoting and supporting an idea, person, activity, service, or cause; persuading people to see the value of an idea, person, activity, or cause; showing enthusiasm and energy about what you believe in; enlisting help and support; spreading a message to a wider audience.

Sales skills

Tasks: Promoting a service or product with the intent of getting someone to buy or accept in exchange for something, usually money; reading the buyer's needs and interests; building confidence and trust with the buyer; anticipating and overcoming objections; explaining and educating the potential buyer about the product or service; closing the sale.

Marketing skills

Tasks: Strategically planning how to present a product or service to the marketplace; identifying who is the market, where they are, and how to reach them; determining how to package and present the product or service to the potential buyer; planning efforts that precede the actual *sale*.

Public relations skills

Tasks: Serving as a representative of an organization to the community at large or to special populations; establishing and maintaining lines of communication between the organization and outside entities; promoting its mission, goals, and/or business efforts.

Teaching and training skills

Tasks: Identifying skills, knowledge, and attitudes needing improvement; breaking down information to be learned in sequential, manageable parts; motivating individuals to learn; soliciting feedback; evaluating learning so as to reintroduce information, if needed; enlightening and explaining.

Counselling skills

Tasks: Guiding and advising; assisting with the identification of personal or work problems and developing strategies to overcome those problems; dealing with the more intense and personal side of people; serving as a support and adviser for individuals.

Analysing skills

Tasks: Breaking a problem, idea, or activity into its component parts; identifying and describing each part and determining how it relates to the other parts; analysis can be applied to people (*how they think, feel, and act*), ideas, activities, information, projects, etc. Being analytical does not necessarily mean being objective.

Problem-solving skills

Tasks: Identifying the key issues or factors in a problem or situation; generating ideas and solutions to solve the problem, selecting the best approach, testing and evaluating it, and selecting another solution if needed; problem solving can be applied to people problems, information and data, or activities and projects; problem solving uses analytical skills.

Programme-development skills

Tasks: Organizing and coordinating a project or programme; involves generating ideas, enlisting help, scheduling, accessing resources, planning the implementation of activities, and overseeing and assisting with the implementation; may or may not require creating ideas or conceptualizing the project.

Curriculum-development skills

Tasks: Designing and developing a learning programme; breaking a body of knowledge into easy-to-learn parts; sequencing information; developing teaching and learning techniques; locating resources and materials; pacing the introduction of information; developing or locating instructional materials.

Instructional-design skills

Tasks: Developing instructional materials; putting ideas into graphic or auditory form; using audio-visual equipment; developing materials for use on audio and visual equipment; using various media to convey ideas and concepts for learning.

Transferable skills

> *When love and skill work together, expect a masterpiece.*
> *John Ruskin*

Look at the following list of transferable skills. Place a tick (✓) by those you possess. Put a star (★) by those you enjoy using.

—— Research and	—— Organizing and
—— Information-Gathering	Implementing
—— Communication	—— Planning and Policy
—— Management	Development
—— Leadership	—— Creating and Developing
—— Interpersonal	—— Promoting
—— Sales	—— Analysing
—— Marketing	—— Problem Solving
—— Public Relations	—— Programme Development
—— Teaching and Training	—— Curriculum Development
—— Counselling	—— Instructional Design

Case Study

Melinda Sharpe, one of our clients who was a registered nurse, went to work for a large pharmaceutical company in customer service. She manages the employees who answer questions from customers. By changing careers, Melinda wasn't able to use her technical nursing skills in her new field of work. However, she did take her personal and transferable skills with her. The transferable skills she acquired as a nurse – problem solving, communication, and interpersonal skills – helped her tremendously as a customer-service manager.

Get in touch with your preferred skills

Have you identified more skills than you thought you had before you began this chapter? We're sure you have. But it isn't enough to know that you possess all of these various skills. We all have a range of skills which we can use, but to be most challenged and satisfied in your work, you need to be operating on preferred skills. Preferred skills are those skills you enjoy using, skills which give you the most payoff. Do you get to use, on a daily basis, all of the skills you put a star next to? They are your preferred skills.

> *Every child is an artist. The problem is how to remain an artist once he grows up.*
>
> *Pablo Picasso*

Why use your preferred skills?

If you work a standard forty-hour week, you will invest 2,040 hours a year in work. We suggest that you ought to be working at something that allows you to take advantage of your preferred skills. Too many people get hung up on staying in careers they don't enjoy, just because they are skilled at those careers. The fact that you can do something well doesn't mean that you have to do it.

Having the opportunity to use your preferred skills is the key to career success. You can't compete with someone who loves his or her work if you don't, and people who love their work are operating on preferred skills. We often ask the participants in our workshops what their days feel like if they get to operate on their preferred skills. They say things like: 'The days go quickly, I don't watch the clock, and I look forward to Mondays.'

Preferred skills are those skills we use naturally and easily; they draw us to certain tasks, activities, and responsibilities. You'll always know when you are using your preferred skills because it feels good. The tasks you want to do first are most often those that involve your preferred skills. And if you look at times when you procrastinate and put work off, you will frequently find that you are facing tasks which involve skills you don't prefer.

How do you develop preferred skills?

Preferred skills are skills you were born with. You may have become better at them, but your preferred skills are innate abilities that you have always had. Many of our clients are unsure about which of their skills are preferred skills. We advise them to think about how they played as children. It's a great indicator of your preferred skills.

How did you play as a child? What did you do for leisure activities in school? Did you read, write, organize groups, draw, or do crafts? Did you negotiate between friends and with family members? If your parents are still alive, ask them how you played. Interview your siblings and/ or friends you played with. If possible, talk to the kids you went to school with and any teachers who are still around.

Additionally, you can check out photographs, home movies, or videos. Give yourself time to think about this. The answer doesn't always come at once. From the time we were little, we used to play school. We'd organize the neighbourhood kids in desks, give them handouts, and teach. Kids used to come to our school after school. Years later, we taught school and then found our niche in teaching people how to find careers that were right for them.

Case Study

A participant in one of our workshops was thinking about becoming an entrepreneur. Our suggestion to think about childhood play experiences jogged her memory. 'Apparently I should be an entrepreneur,' she said, 'because I set up my own school and charged kids a penny to teach them to read. I did make money, but that's not the whole story,' she remarked. 'I was only four years old, and I, myself, didn't know how to read.'

As a child, a woman who now owns a large yogourt franchise made mud pies that looked like chocolate and sold them to people. The wife of a gentleman who owns a chain of exclusive grocery stores, told us that her husband constantly tells stories about playing shops as a kid. And a structural engineer recounted how he used to take apart his toys to see how they worked and rebuilt them. Delve back into your past and answer the following questions.

1.   What positive feedback (*from parents, coaches, teachers, and family*) did you get as a child?

_____

_____

_____

_____

_____

_____

2.   How did you play as a child or an adolescent?

_____

_____

_____

_____

_____

3.   Describe something you did on a volunteer basis that you really enjoyed.

_____

_____

_____

_____

4.   Describe a task or activity that you love to do (*one that you gravitate to naturally*).

_____

_____

_____

_____

_____

_____

Case Study

One of our clients, Patricia Milford, told us she was preparing to go to law school. 'Why?' we asked. 'Do you have some innate desire to be a barrister?' 'No, I don't,' she replied. 'I just want to work.' We discovered that while Patricia wasn't currently employed, she was involved in major volunteer work. 'I helped organize the big American Dental Association conventions in Chicago.' 'For free?' we asked. 'Sure,' she replied. 'We're a volunteer group.' 'Then you have a career,' we told her. 'You just haven't put a label on it. You're a meeting-and-events planner. You apparently have an innate preferred skill of organizing events, people, and happenings.' Patricia now owns a very successful meeting-and-events planning business, and she contracts to professional organizations and companies to put on major sales events, conferences, and conventions.

Tapping into your preferred skills

Not everyone finds it easy to determine their preferred skills. If you are having difficulty, you might try what we tell our clients. One suggestion we have is to get feedback from others about your skills. Ask five people you know and trust to tell you what your skills are. Ask them: 'What am I particularly good at?'

We also often ask clients to write accomplishment stories and pull out the skills they find in those stories. To do this, you must begin documenting your accomplishments and successes. Then you will write a work-related accomplishment story and a non-work-related story.

> *You need to claim the events of your life to make yourself yours.*
> Anne-Wilson Schaef

An accomplishment is something you did that gave you real satisfaction and that you felt was successful. Include all the tasks you completed that were related to that accomplishment. Some examples of accomplishments are:

- a mother who prepares her young family to be self-sufficient during her operation;

- starting a family tradition;

- writing a newsletter;

- serving as an elected officer of a club;

- winning a speech contest in secondary school;

- initiating a new tracking system for inventory at work;

- lobbying the local authority to put in a stop sign at a dangerous intersection.

Are you getting the idea? You can list accomplishments from childhood, adolescence, young adulthood, or adulthood. It's a valuable and gratifying activity.

After you have finished writing the stories, you will need to read between the lines to identify the skills you used in the situations. List all the skills, qualities, and traits you used in accomplishing the tasks. From this list will emerge your personal and transferable skills. Look at the following two examples; then write your own stories.

Work-related accomplishment story: 'Organizing a task force'

Work-related accomplishment story	Skills I exhibited
My manager came back from a meeting and asked me to organize a task force to look at the issue of employee turnover. I first brainstormed with my boss the five other people who needed to be on the task force and I set up the initial meeting.	Persuasive Self-starting Interpersonal Cooperative Organizing
At the initial meeting, I led the group in setting the task force's mission, goals, and objectives. The group spent thirty minutes debating the causes for turnover; and, when I saw we weren't getting anywhere, I suggested we create a method for collecting data on why employees left. We created the methodology and agreed on the tasks to be done for the next meeting. We ended the meeting on time and set the dates for subsequent meetings.	Leading Goal-Oriented Communicating Resolving Conflicts Diplomatic Creating Action-Oriented Managing Meetings

Now write your own work-related accomplishment story and indentify the skills you used.

Work-related accomplishment story	Skills I exhibited

Non-work-related accomplishment story:
'planning my parents' 50th anniversary party'

Non-work-related accomplishment story	Skills I exhibited
I thought we should surprise my parents for their 50th anniversary party, so I called my two sisters to help.	Planning
We set up a meeting and laid out the plans. I created the invitation and had it designed and hand-printed by a calligrapher. I asked the guests to bring a picture and a memory to share, in lieu of purchasing gifts. I found a way to take my parents' address books (old and new), so that I could invite both recent and old friends. I also planned the menu and found two neighbourhood women to do the cooking and the catering. My sisters took care of the decorating and getting my parents to the party.	Creating Organizing Enthusiastic Interpersonal Thoughtful Detail-Oriented Communicating
My parents were surprised, and everyone had a great time. The memories and pictures were very touching and my parents got to see friends they hadn't seen in years.	Persuasion Delegating

Write your own non-work-related accomplishment story and identify the skills you used. Often you can uncover your preferred skills in non-work-related accomplishments, because they're usually not something you 'had to do'.

Non-work-related accomplishment story	Skills I exhibited

By now, you should have a better idea of both the skills you possess and which of those skills you prefer to use. You'll know what you bring to the table. Perhaps you have many skills you don't even use in your current job, skills you'd really like to utilize. Knowing what you can do well and what you prefer to do lets you look at your career in a whole new light. You're not far off from unlocking your career potential.

Conclusion

The skills you bring to a job are varied. They consist of technical, personal, and transferable skills. Most likely, however, you are using skills you prefer not to use and not using skills you'd like to. How do you get around this dilemma? You pinpoint the skills you possess, and then determine which of those are your preferred skills. It's rewarding to analyse and reflect on the things you both do well and enjoy, because it provides you with exciting insights into what you should do to have a fulfilling career.

'With McBride here as our fall-back, our systems are virtually fool-proof.'

CHAPTER SEVEN

Determining Where Money Fits

Key points

 Rethinking your relationship with money may free you to make better career decisions.

 What you need is different from what you want, although many people confuse the two.

 It's easier to make future job or career decisions if you know what it really costs you to go to work.

 Financial independence may be more attainable than you think, and it's definitely worth pursuing.

We know what you may be thinking. 'Aha!' you're saying to yourself. 'I was just getting excited, learning about my desires and my skills. I've decided that I need to make a career change, but I'll bet they're going to dash my dreams in this chapter, because I may not be able to make the change and support my lifestyle at the same time.' Wrong! That's not the premise of this chapter. On the other hand, we're not about to tell you that you should go ahead and do whatever you want and the money will fall in line. We wish that were true, but it's not quite that easy.

We would like to challenge you, get you to re-configure your notions about money and move you as close as possible to doing exactly what you'd like to do. The challenge involves thinking carefully about what you really need and realizing the true cost of working. We have found it to be liberating, and many of our clients have also. Check it out for yourself.

> *Work is the rent we pay for living on this planet.*
> *The Queen Mother*

Are you courting money, married to it, or in the midst of divorcing it?

How would you describe your relationship with money? Maybe you feel that it is relatively objective. Money comes into your life via a paycheck, and you methodically portion it out according to the number of bills you receive each month. But absolutely no one has a sterile relationship with money. It's usually a complicated relationship that has evolved over time.

Where do you get your relationship with money?

The same place you got your attitudes about work – from your parents. Think about it. Did you ever hear your parents talk about money? Perhaps they let drop little pearls of wisdom, like:

- the love of money is the root of all evil;
- a penny saved is a penny earned;
- money does not grow on trees;
- money does not buy happiness.

Usually these sayings were brought out when you asked for something they didn't want you to have. But your parents did pass on their relationship with money to you, and you responded in one of two ways. You either swallowed it hook, line, and sinker, or you rebelled. You had thrifty parents, and you either became a tightwad or a spendaholic. Or your parents spent money freely, and you responded in kind or revolted. It can go either way.

> **Case Study**
>
> *A participant in one of our workshops shared her obsession with money, which came about as a result of her background. 'I was raised in a house where my parents pinched pennies,' she said. 'We had money, but they never spent it. It made no sense to me, because I was denied many reasonable requests for money.' As a result, this lady made a 180-degree turn in her own relationship with money. 'I have done the exact opposite of my parents. I can't deny my kids anything,' she said. 'My credit cards are close to their limits, and I spend my raises before I get them. I know it's very dysfunctional, but I can't seem to change.'*

What messages did you hear about money and its value?

_____

_____

_____

_____

_____

_____

_____

_____

_____

_____

_____

_____

What is your relationship with money?

Our relationship with money is far more complex than we usually assume. Consider that the number-one, unresolved issue in marriage is money, and you begin to understand the necessity for a healthy relationship with money. We've heard from many unmarried folks that they struggle with it, too.

What is your relationship with money? Do you feel like you handle your money well? Do you feel in control of it? Do you feel you know what money can and cannot do for you? Place yourself on the money continuum. Mark an X on the spot that describes your relationship with money.

Unhealthy   *Average*   *Healthy*   *Very Healthy*

Describe your relationship with money. Does your relationship with money reflect your parents' relationship, or have you formed a different relationship?

_____

_____

_____

_____

_____

_____

The issue of money is quite relevant to career decisions, because most people make career decisions with money in mind. Conventional wisdom uses money as a benchmark for success – 'You're only successful if you make a lot of money, and you can only be happy in your career if you make loads of it.' Rubbish! Some people feel that way, but you'll be extremely unhappy if you follow that road. More people place money in the middle of their career lists. They think it's important, but it doesn't take precedence over their desire to do something they enjoy.

Case Study

One of our clients found himself in a dilemma. He got into sales because of the lure of a six-figure income, but it wasn't what he wanted to do. 'I detest sales,' he told us. 'And the money doesn't help all that much. I spend it just to anaesthetize my bad feelings about the job. I purchased a new home and a luxury car. And I go on expensive holidays to get away from my job. Now I'm stuck,' he said. 'I can't leave a job I hate, because I'll lose my house and my car. No other job I can get will pay enough to support my lifestyle.'

Your needs versus your wants

People continually confuse their wants and their needs; and, since most wants and needs are inextricably tied to money, it's an issue that must be addressed if you want to establish a healthier relationship with money. Most people think they need something that much more closely resembles a want. If you are considering a career or job change, you should get in touch with your true wants and needs.

Many people think that they have to make a certain amount of money. Because they're so focused on that magic number, they don't allow themselves to make creative or passionate career decisions. If there is something you have always wanted to do, but it means starting over or making less money than you do now, it is especially important that you identify your wants and needs.

All we have to do is ask people what they need, and they find it easy to list their desires. 'I need to make £60,000 a year,' one person told us. 'I need to drive a Mercedes,' said another. 'I need a 4 bedroom detached home with an acre of land right next to the beach,' says another. 'Hold on,' we say. 'Your needs sound suspiciously like wants.' Are you in the habit of doing the same?

> *We act as though comfort and luxury were the chief requirements of life, when all that we need to make us happy is something to be enthusiastic about.*
>
> *Charles Kingsley*

Needs are more general. They don't imply something quantifiable, nor do they refer to a particular label or status symbol. Fulfilling your needs means that you are satisfied, not ecstatic. While you may *want* to make £60,000 a year, your *need* is to be free from financial worries. That huge house is a want, while a home with a pleasant environment is a need. You may drool when you see a Mercedes, but you need to drive a vehicle that won't break down. Wants box you in; needs leave the options open.

Look at the following list of examples. Then make a list of what you need versus what you want. Place a star (*) next to your top five (5) needs.

Needs	*Wants*
• Time for physical exercise	• Membership in an exclusive gym
• An appealing, comfortable, and safe home environment	• A 4 bedroom detached home by the beach
• Freedom from financial worries	• Earn at least £60,000 a year
• New, stimulating surroundings	• An around-the-world trip
• Time to be with my children	• A holiday home in the Caribbean
• A good laugh at least once a day	• A trip to Disney World for the whole family
• Interesting work and mental stimulation	• A promotion and more money
• Time alone to pursue my art	• Art classes in Paris
• Acceptance for who I am (from me)	• My mother's approval

Needs	Wants

Fulfilling your needs is much easier than supplying your wants. And it just may be that you can fulfil all of your needs, even if you desire a job or career that pays less than your current one.

When is enough 'enough'?

The confusion surrounding needs and wants fuels a desire to spend, spend, spend. Let's say that you make £20,000 a year, and it's not quite enough. So you say to yourself, 'I have to struggle on this salary, but when I make £30,000, life will be great.' And eventually you make £30,000 a year.

Before long, you're saying, 'I can't make ends meet. I need to make £35,000 a year. Then life will be great.' But it won't, because by the time you make £35,000, it won't be enough.

We all operate on this level to some degree. There's always something else out there to spend your money on. That's what keeps people in debt and working. We've all heard the saying: *I owe, I owe, it's off to work I go*, and unfortunately, it hits a little bit too close to home.

How do you get out of this mess?

Look carefully at what you spend your money on. If you have the desire to keep a diary of all your expenditures for a month or longer, by all means do so. It may be quite an eye-opener for you. If you'd rather not, try to be more aware of how you spend your money. A participant in one of our workshops discovered that he spent hundreds of dollars on magazine and newsletter subscriptions, many of which went unread. 'I've decided to stick with the one newsletter and two magazines I read. The others I can borrow from the library if I want to,' he said. 'I've figured that this one change will save me one hundred pounds a year.'

> **Case Study**
>
> We had one client who, until she paid attention to her finances, didn't realize that the low-fat muffin and gourmet cup of coffee she purchased every morning cost her £15 a week. When she calculated the yearly charge – £750 – she gave the muffins a miss and brought a flask of coffee from home. 'The money I save will go towards paying off my credit card,' she said. 'And my goal is a balance of zero within eighteen months.'

Look at the five needs you put a star next to in the exercise you just completed. Can you fulfil those needs without breaking your budget or without needing to find a job that pays you more than you currently earn? Maybe you need to buy a car. Instead of purchasing the car of your dreams (a *want*), you could opt for purchasing a used model of a car you like.

Such choices may free you from being tied to a career you don't enjoy or perhaps from having to work overtime to afford items you want, but don't really need. Before you make any purchase, ask yourself: 'Is this purchase worth my time and my effort?' Why ask yourself this? Because the money you hand over represents hard work and energy – the hours you spend at work.

One of our clients illustrated this concept well when he told us, 'I was writing out a cheque for seven hundred pounds at a home electronics store, preparing to purchase a new stereo system for my car, when I suddenly stopped and tore it up. The assistant looked at me in surprise. I apologized to her, then explained, "I have a perfectly good system in my car already. This isn't worth sixty hours of work."'

Once you figure out exactly what you make per hour at work, you too can determine whether any purchase you make is worth the hours you invest at your job or in your career.

What's your current financial picture?

You may make £50,000 a year and not be further ahead of someone who makes £35,000. Why? Because the hidden cost of work may be more expensive for you. The £35,000 worker may not have to purchase high-priced work clothes, spend pounds in commuting every day, nor pay for child-care costs. It all depends on your job or career, and what you have to pay to work there.

How much does it cost you to go to work? Without knowing the true cost of going to your job, it is difficult to make future job or career decisions. Complete the following worksheet to determine what it costs you to go to work.

What does it cost me to go to work?

Enter your yearly cost for each category. For example, list how much you spend on petrol, daycare, or breakfast in the course of a year. Not all categories will apply to you. Enter costs for those that do, and try to be as accurate as possible.

—— **Commuting costs**
Petrol
Maintenance
Parking
—— **Clothing/accessories**
Clothes worn only to work
Dry-cleaning
Shoes/purses/briefcase
—— **Meals**
Breakfast
Lunch
Dinner
Tea/Snacks
—— **Daycare/child care**

—— **Goods and services you buy because you are so busy**
Cleaning
Gardening
Car-washing
Convenience foods
Etc.
—— **Education and training**
Conferences
Classes
Professional associations

Total £ spent every year: ——————

Case Study

Brenda White, one of our clients, made £23.00 an hour at her job, a job which required a long, daily commute. We explained the concept of determining your true hourly rate, and Brenda filled out the worksheet. After she threw in all her hidden costs – child care, car and commuting expenses, home maintenance, food, clothes, etc, she discovered that she made only £7.00 an hour. Brenda decided to open a home-based business. She takes care of her own kids, is free from her long commute, and makes £14.00 an hour after expenses, which is quite a bit more than her £23.00-an-hour job.

I have enough money to last me the rest of my life if I don't buy something.

Jackie Mason

Once you have calculated your yearly cost of going to work, deduct it from what you make in one year. This number is what you really make in one year. Then go one step further and divide your *real* salary by the number of hours you work in a year to get your true hourly rate. Don't forget to count all the hours you work. Add in unpaid overtime. We even go so far as to tell clients to factor in the hours they spend commuting, because that's all part of your work hours. A person commuting two hours daily adds ten hours to his or her weekly work schedule. A home-based worker doesn't add any.

Yearly salary – yearly cost of going to work ÷ number of hours you work in one year = your true hourly rate.

Is your true hourly rate a disappointment? If you just shaved seven pounds off your fourteen pound wage, you might feel cheated. Don't. Knowing what you really make leaves you open to new options in the world of work. Maybe you felt you could never switch to a career you liked, because the pay cut wouldn't cut it with your family. Now you realize that it's a possibility. Other alternatives:

- Could you find a position closer to home? You'll save money in commuting costs, and you will save time.

- Could you find a less-demanding position (*time-wise*) to free up time to do things for yourself?

- What about finding a work environment that is less formal, and therefore less expensive to be in?

- How about working at home? You could save money in child-care costs, commuting expenses, clothing, etc.

Freedom at last

We believe that the greatest gift you can give to your children or yourself is the ability to *live below your means*, to not spend all the money you make. Most people are searching for ways to live within their means, because they always end up living above their means. If you analyse your needs and wants, and consider all of your purchases before you make them, you may be able to live below your means. And just think of the career freedom you will have if you consistently *live below your means*.

We conducted a career counselling workshop at a major organization that was downsizing. The room was packed with engineers who knew their days were numbered, and they were nervous, depressed, and full of anxiety. All except for one, a man by the name of Tim Hart. We asked Tim why he wasn't visibly upset. Tim told us that he had no debts, not even a mortgage. 'The last payment I made on my house was five years ago,' Tim recounted. 'At that time, my colleagues made fun of me. They said I was foolish for getting rid of my tax deduction. Now they aren't laughing. I'm not worried about losing my job. I could get a job at a fast-food restaurant if I wanted, or not even work at all, because I don't need to earn money.' When we asked Tim how he did it, he said that he never increased his spending. 'If I got a raise, I paid extra payments to my mortgage company. The same with my bonuses. I didn't find it that difficult to do.'

We're not telling you that you won't or can't make lots of money. We just advise people not to get into a position where they have to make lots of money. Because then you may have to sacrifice your wants and desires concerning work environment, who you want to work with, and the use of your preferred skills. You don't want to be trapped in a position, just because you're deep in debt.

What most people are working for is the opportunity not to work – the opportunity to be financially independent. Most people expect to be financially independent at retirement age, but even many retirees are finding it difficult to make it on Social Security and pension plans. What is financial independence? We like to define it as 'having an income sufficient for your basic needs and comforts from a source other than paid employment.' Wouldn't you like to be financially independent long before you turn 65?

While there are many roads to financial independence, the surest way for all of us – no matter who we work for or how much we earn – is to get out of short-term debt (*credit cards*) and long-term debt (*mortgages*) and decide what we really need to make us happy. Often, when you are clear about where your money goes, what it costs you to go to work, and what you can really expect to get in return for a specific purchase, you are on your way to managing your money and living below your means. And doing so opens up all kinds of career options for you.

> *Being tied to money is financial slavery. Learn to free yourself from its bonds.*
>
> *Peggy Boedecker*

Conclusion

The issue of money is a loaded one, full of preconceptions and complexities. If you can focus on your relationship with money and understand what it can and can't do for you, you will begin to treat money in a healthy manner. Maintaining a healthy relationship with money involves analysing your needs and wants, coming to grips with what your true hourly rate is, and determining whether you can live below your means. If you're willing and able to do all this, you may be on your way to financial independence and a whole new world of career opportunities.

CHAPTER EIGHT

Opening the Door to Career Options, Opportunities, and Choices

Key points

 Now that you have the keys to unlocking your career potential, you have the option of using them.

 Completing a career checklist and an *Ideal Day* activity will enable you to come up with career opportunities that are right for you.

We've given you a lot to think about. If you've read all the previous chapters in this book, you should be much clearer about what you want from a career, what you have to offer, and how you can adjust your finances to accommodate your preferences. In this chapter, you'll pull all the insights you've uncovered into one succinct checklist; additionally, you'll complete an *Ideal Day* activity, which will explore your desires concerning work. Together, the checklist and activity may prove to be the catalyst that cracks open your career potential.

Using the keys to unlock your career potential

You now have the keys in your hand. Some will be more important to you, based on your current desires; others may become critical at later stages in your life. That's the benefit of having these exercises. You can refer back to them at any time. So don't get rid of this book; in ten years, when you're in the midst of a career crisis, you may need to redo the activities and see how your needs, desires, and skills have changed.

A former client, Stephen Longridge, contacted us to report how he recently had used his career notebook to track changes. We had counselled him eight years previously. At that time, Stephen was working as an assistant buyer for a computer manufacturer. The job was just a job, he had told us, one he had fallen into because he needed work. Stephen analysed his needs, his desires, and his skills, and he completely switched fields, finding work as a graphic artist. 'I enjoyed the work tremendously,' he said, 'but when I happened upon my career notebook and filled out the activity sheets all over again, I realized I had changed. I wanted a different environment, a shorter commute, and more independence in choosing my projects. I opened my own home-based business,' he said. 'And I'm much happier.'

Create your career checklist

Your career checklist is not set in stone. It's based on your motivations, desires, needs, and skills at this particular point in your life. Look over the checklist; then read through the examples given. In creating your own checklist, be as specific as you can, and as wordy as you'd like.

Career checklist

Understanding Why You Work As You Do: Where does work fit into your life?

_____
_____
_____

Deciding Where You Belong: What or where is your ideal environment?

_____
_____
_____

Knowing Who To Work With: What is your ideal balance between people, data, and things? Who do you enjoy working with and in what way?

_____
_____
_____

Looking At What You Bring To The Table: What are your preferred skills?

_____
_____
_____

Determining Where Money Fits: Are you getting the financial reward you need or want? Are you headed towards financial independence?

_____
_____

Options: _____

Case Study 1: Mary Winston Age : 45   Occupation: Administrative Assistant

Career checklist

Understanding Why You Work As You Do: Where does work fit into your life?

I grew up in a family where everyone just had a job – so I did too. Now that I'm 45, and my kids are in secondary school, I want more. I think I'm ready for a career. I have more time, so I'm going back to adult education to finish my degree.

Deciding Where You Belong: What or where is your ideal environment?

I enjoy the large environment that I'm in. I know there's really no security, but I like an organization that has been around a long-time, and I like being part of the energy industry. I feel good about being associated with an organization that everyone recognizes.

Knowing Who To Work With: What is your ideal balance between people, data, and things? Who do you enjoy working with and in what way?

I can see that I could use more people interaction. I enjoy my colleagues and our clients. I'm going to see if I can work on a couple of projects that would allow me more teamwork.

Looking At What You Bring To The Table: What are your skills?

I always knew I had good personal skills. I would like to move away from my technical skills (word processing) and use more of my transferable skills. I've done a lot of volunteer work where I've played a leadership role. I am ready to use those skills at work.

Determining Where Money Fits: Are you getting the financial reward you need or want? Are you headed towards financial independence?

I feel that I'm adequately compensated for my work. I'm a good money manager, but I can see that I will have to get better as the organization cuts back on our benefits. I'd like to start my own retirement fund, in case I need it.

Options.

I would like to get into management. I'm thinking about visiting our human resources department, because I've always been interested in doing that kind of work. I'm also going to talk to someone in our new customer-service centre. As I finish my degree, I'm going to watch the job advertising system for opportunities. Meanwhile, I've shared my goals and insights with my manager, and she's going to give me new opportunities.

Case Study 2: Dan Moreton Age : 37   Occupation: Manager of Technical Support

Career checklist

Understanding Why You Work As You Do: Where does work fit into your life?

I have always been very career oriented. I've been working since I was 16 and very rarely take a holiday. Work is still important to me, but I am ready for a change. I still need the challenge and creativity, but I don't want it to be so all-consuming. My kids are 8 and 10, and I really want to participate in their lives.

Deciding Where You Belong: What or where is your ideal environment?

I've always worked in large organizations. I have made good progress going through their ranks, but I am really tired of the bureaucracy and approval channels. I like the computer industry, but would like a smaller organization. I visited a small, international manufacturing firm last week, because I coach Junior Football with the owner. There were no private offices, and everyone was dressed in casual clothes and jeans. I don't know if I'm ready for such a big change, but I'm tired of this.

Knowing Who To Work With: What is your ideal balance between people, data, and things? Who do you enjoy working with and in what way?

I've always been very technically competent and 'good with people.' That's led me into supervisory and management positions. I've discovered that I can manage people, but I really don't want to. I don't mind leading a project, but I'd like to get out of day-to-day management. I also need to take a couple of technical classes to make sure I stay up-to-date.

Looking At What You Bring To The Table: What are your skills?

I bring excellent interpersonal and communicating skills. I'm highly organized and love to manage projects from beginning to end.

Determining Where Money Fits: Are you getting the financial reward you need or want? Are you headed towards financial independence?

If I leave this big organization and don't look for a management position, I need to anticipate some cut in income, at least for a while. In my experience, small organizations pay as well or better, but don't have such elaborate benefit packages. My wife and I are working on eliminating our short-term debt and reducing our long-term debt. I understand that the less debt I have, the more options I have. One of these days, I'd like to work for myself in a home-based business.

Options:
I'd like to do what I am doing now, either:
- *in a smaller organization as an individual contributor, but not as a manager;*
- *as a subcontractor with several organizations as my clients.*

Case Study 3: Linda Reynolds Age : 30 Occupation: University tutor

Career checklist

Understanding Why You Work As You Do: Where does work fit into your life?

I am working as hard as I can as a university tutor, and I want to remain career-oriented. I am no longer motivated by academic work and am not interested in another degree (I have a Masters). I've enjoyed the flexibility that teaching has given me, but I'm ready for something new.

Deciding Where You Belong: What or where is your ideal environment?

I have been in the educational arena my entire career. I am interested in exploring both the government and business area. I would like a much smaller environment than a red brick university. It is very difficult to have an impact here. I am also ready for a more business-like environment and wouldn't mind dressing up every day.

Knowing Who To Work With: What is your ideal balance between people, data, and things? Who do you enjoy working with and in what way?

I like a balance of people and data (about 50/50). I love reading books, developing programmes, and training or leading people.

Looking At What You Bring To The Table: What are your skills?

I like analysing situations to see how things could run more efficiently and how people could work together in more harmony.

Determining Where Money Fits: Are you getting the financial reward you need or want? Are you headed towards financial independence?

I am very interested in making more money and testing my value. Many of my colleagues have told me you can't do valuable work if you're motivated by money, but I don't think that's true. Not making money has always given me the excuse for not managing my money well, so I know I need to learn to do this, too.

Options:

I am looking at three possible careers. First, I am going to talk to a friend of a friend who is the assistant to one of our county councillors. Then I am going to visit the training department of a large corporation. Last, I am going to talk to an organizational-development consultant who is part of a consulting group.

Describe your ideal day

The following *Ideal Day* activity will help you pinpoint more career desires, needs, motivations, and skills. It may stimulate you to come up with more ideas; the least it will do is allow you to describe your career ideals to others.

The ideal day

1. My alarm clock rings at _____. Since I usually work about _____ hours, I will finish my work day at _____.

2. The activity that gets my day going well is _____ _____.

3. As I walk out the door, I look at myself in the mirror, and I see _____ _____.

4. To get to work, I (*kind of transportation*) _____ _____.

5. The place I work is (*describe it and what it is near*) _____ _____.

6. The first part of my morning is spent _____ _____.

7. I enjoy making use of (*machines, equipment, books, skills*)_____ _____.

8. I prefer (*tick one*) to ___ not to ___ take a break before lunch. My idea of a break is usually _____ _____.

9. In the time left until lunch, I _____ _____.

10. For lunch, I (*Where did you go? With whom? What did you eat?*) _____
    _____.

11. Who paid for lunch? _____
    _____.

12. When I returned to work, I spent my time _____
    _____.

13. Someone just stepped into my office. It is _____
    _____ who is here to/for: _____
    _____.

14. I just had a meeting with my superior. I have been offered a promotion to _____
    _____, which enables me to _____.

15. I don't have a superior. Instead I just met with (*tick one*) my partner/associate _____ or a client/customer, _____ and we will be taking a new step, which is _____
    _____.

16. It has been a rewarding day, because I have used the skill I most enjoy using, which is _____
    _____.

17. Today is payday. I get paid every _____ by (*cheque, cash, money order, etc.*) _____, and I earn £_____.

18. As I prepare to leave work, I _____
    _____.

19. Next week will be (*tick one or more*) interesting ____
    _____ exciting _____ challenging
    _____ relaxing _____ lucrative, _____ because _____
    _____.

20. After I leave my place of work, I _____
_____.

21. This evening, I will _____
_____.

22. This has been a fantastic day. The part I enjoyed the most
was _____
_____.

List the five most important items that appear in your
total day.

1. _____

2. _____

3. _____

4. _____

5. _____

Now that you are back in the *real world*, review your
responses to the twenty-two items and: (1) put a check by
those which you now have in your current job; (2) put a star
by those that you think you can achieve in your current job
if you try; and (3) circle those that you can only achieve by
changing your career or your present position. In which
category do your top five appear?

What do you do now?

Creating your career checklist and describing your ideal day
won't do anything for you, unless you do something with
them. If you have discovered through the exercises and

activities in this book that you are perfectly happy where you are presently, then you can store the checklist and activity, and retake them at a later date when you feel ready for a change. You will have satisfied your urge to see if a change was necessary.

More likely, you have uncovered needs that aren't being met in your current position or preferred skills that aren't being utilized, or maybe you have discovered that a different environment would better complement your personality and work style. Whatever your career checklist and *Ideal Day* activity reveal, you can either put them on the shelf or use them to your advantage. We suggest that you use them.

If you're in a state of *analysis paralysis,* and are having difficulty coming up with ideas of what to do, we give you the following suggestions:

- Look carefully at your checklist and *Ideal Day* activity, and note any ideas that pop into your mind. Many of our clients write little notes to themselves as they are going through their checklists, such as 'What about a position in marketing?' or 'I'd be interested in telecommuting or working at home' or 'Check out courses in computer literacy'. Doing so makes adding to the *options* part of your checklist much easier.

- Take a look at your own job and see where you can make changes. Many people find they only need to make minor adjustments to their own careers to be satisfied. One client negotiated a change in tasks – she dropped the writing of some detailed reports and took on some committee projects instead. Another client asked to move to a quieter cubicle. The change in environment made it easier for him to complete his work.

- See if there's a job within your organization that matches your career checklist and approximates to the description of your ideal day. Maybe you're in production and your checklist reveals that you'd do better in sales. Check for any internal job openings that correspond with your checklist and activity sheet.

- If your organization is short on the jobs you'd prefer or the environment is totally wrong for you, study the jobs section in the 'Dailies'. Not everyone finds a perfect position in the jobs section, but it is a possible avenue whereby you discover what you've been looking for.

- Share your checklist and the description of your ideal day with four or five people you trust and ask them for their suggestions. Sometimes you're too close to the issue to see what's obvious to others.

- Use your checklist and activity sheet to plan for a future career, perhaps a retirement or second career. One of our clients enjoyed his work as an engineer, but decided that when he retired, he would like to pursue a career that involved the growing and harvesting of herbs. 'And thanks to your ideas for achieving financial independence,' he told us, 'I'll get to pursue that career much earlier than I would have anticipated.'

Ideas won't keep. Something must be done about them.
Alfred North Whitehead

If you have determined that a job or career switch is on the cards, it's in your best interest to learn how to market yourself and how to successfully manoeuvre a career transition. Check out books on these topics. We've published *Marketing Yourself and Your Career* and *Making Career Transitions*.

You own the keys that will unlock your career potential. Use them to open the door to new opportunities. Your career checklist and *Ideal Day* activity will get you thinking about how you can work yourself into a job or career that's right for you. Swing that career door open and enter an exciting world.

Conclusion

You're at the end of the discovery process. What you have learnt about yourself in this book you have captured in your career checklist and in your *Ideal Day* activity. What have you discovered? Will you change nothing, tweak some specifics within your current position, switch to a different department, or head for a totally new career or job elsewhere? Choose what's best for you. And remember: whenever you feel that another change is in order, recheck the keys to unlocking your career potential. They'll work for the rest of your life.

TITLES CURRENTLY AVAILABLE IN THE PERSONAL GROWTH AND DEVELOPMENT COLLECTION

Managing Your Career in a Changing Workplace

Unlocking Your Career Potential

Marketing Yourself and Your Career

Making Career Transitions

WORKSHOPS

Dynamic and interactive in-house and public workshops are available from Richard Chang Associates, Inc. on a variety of personal, professional, and organizational development topics.

ADDITIONAL RESOURCES FROM RICHARD CHANG ASSOCIATES, INC. PUBLICATIONS DIVISION

PRACTICAL GUIDEBOOK COLLECTION

Available through Richard Chang Associates, Inc., fine bookstores, and training and organizational development resource catalogues worldwide.

QUALITY IMPROVEMENT SERIES
Continuous Process Improvement
Continuous Improvement Tools Volume 1
Continuous Improvement Tools Volume 2
Step-By-Step Problem Solving
Meetings That Work!
Improving Through Benchmarking
Succeeding As A Self-Managed Team
Satisfying Internal Customers First!
Process Reeingineering In Action
Measuring Organizational Improvement Impact

HIGH-IMPACT TRAINING SERIES
Creating High-Impact Training
Identifying Targeted Training Needs
Mapping A Wining Training Approach
Producing High-Impact Learning Tools
Applying Successful Training Techniques
Measuring The Impact Of Training
Make Your Training Results Last

MANAGEMENT SKILLS SERIES
Coaching Through Effective Feedback
Expanding Leadership Impact
Mastering Change Management
On-The-Job Orientation And Training
Re-Creating Teams During Transitions

WORKPLACE DIVERSITY SERIES
Capitalizing On Workplace Diversity
Successful Staffing In A Diverse Workplace
Team-Building For Diverse Work Groups
Communicating In A Diverse Workplace
Tools For Valuing Diversity

HIGH PERFORMANCE TEAM SERIES
Success Through Teamwork
Building A Dynamic Team
Measuring Team Performance
Team Decision-Making Techniques

101 STUPID THINGS SERIES
101 Stupid Things Trainers Do To
  Sabotage Success
101 Stupid Things Supervisors Do To
  Sabotage Success
101 Stupid Things Employees Do To
  Sabotage Success

TRAINING PRODUCTS
Step-By-Step Problem Solving Tool Kit
Meetings That Work! Trainer's Kit
Continuous Improvement Tools Volume 1 Trainer's Kit

VIDEOTAPES (US FORMAT ONLY)
Mastering Change Management**
Quality: You Don't Have To Be Sick To Get Better*
Achieving Results Through Quality Improvement*
Total Quality: Myths, Methods, Or Miracles**
  Featuring Drs. Ken Blanchard and Richard Chang
Empowering The Quality Effort**

  Featuring Drs. Ken Blanchard and Richard Chang

TOTAL QUALITY VIDEO SERIES AND WORKBOOKS
Building Commitment**
Teaming Up**
Applied Problem Solving**
Self-Directed Evaluation**

* Produced by American Media Inc.

** Produced by Double Vision Studios.

EVALUATION AND FEEDBACK FORM

We need your help to continuously improve the quality of the resources provided through the Richard Chang Associates, Inc., Publications Division. We would greatly appreciate your imput and suggestions regarding this particular book, as well as future book interests.

Thank you in advance for your feedback.

Title: _____

1. Overall, how would you rate your *level of satisfaction* with this book? Please circle your response.

   Extremely Dissatisfied   Satisfied   Extremely Satisfied

         1   2   3   4   5

2. What did you find *most* helpful?

   _____

   _____

3. What did you find *least* helpful?

   _____

   _____

4. What *characteristics/features/benefits* are most important to you in making a decision to purchase a book?

   _____

   _____

5. What additional *subject matter/topic areas* would you like to see addressed in future books from Richard Chang Associates, Inc.?

   _____

   _____

Name *(optional):*_____

Address:_____

Post Code _____ **Phone:** (   )_____

PLEASE FAX YOUR RESPONSES TO: (714) 727-7007 (US) or 0171 837 6348 (UK)